I0813350

한식을 넘어서

BEYOND KOREAN

Easy recipes for Korean, Japanese, and Chinese favorites

AARON HUH

creator of Aaron and Claire

Publisher Mike Sanders
Art & Design Director William Thomas
Editorial Director Ann Barton
Editor Brandon Buechley
Senior Designer Jessica Lee
Senior Layout Tech Ayanna Lacey
Photographer Sun Kwon
Food Stylist Hyeseon Shin
Copy Editor Mira S. Park
Proofreader Bianca Bosman
Indexer Beverlee Day

First American Edition, 2025
Published in the United States by DK Publishing
1745 Broadway, 20th Floor, New York, NY 10019

The authorized representative in the EEA is Dorling Kindersley Verlag GmbH. Arnulfstr. 124, 80636 Munich, Germany

25 26 27 28 29 10 9 8 7 6 5 4 3 2 1
001-351203-DEC2025

A catalog record for this book is available from the Library of Congress.
ISBN 979-8-217-12716-0

Printed and bound in China

www.dk.com

This book was made with Forest Stewardship Council™ certified paper – one small step in DK's commitment to a sustainable future.
Learn more at**www.dk.com/uk/information/sustainability**

I dedicate this book to my beloved wife, Claire, and our soon-to-be-born son.

Claire, it was your incredible, unwavering support that made it possible for me to complete this wonderful book. Your endless encouragement has been my greatest source of happiness and inspiration—without you, none of this would have been possible. Thank you from the bottom of my heart. I love you.

And to our son, who will soon join us—thank you for coming into our lives while I was writing this book. You've turned what could have been challenging times into joyful moments. I hope you grow up healthy and strong—I can't wait for the day we cook together using this book. See you soon, buddy.

CONTENTS

DON'T WORRY ABOUT IT!

HELLO (AGAIN) FROM SEOUL!

I'm not going to start this book with boring clichés like, "When I was young..." or "My family used to..." I'm pretty sure you're sick and tired of hearing those predictable stories. So, I promise I won't waste valuable pages of this book on that kind of content.

To me, the true essence of a cookbook lies in providing amazing recipes that readers truly enjoy. So, in this book, I wrote 100 amazing East Asian recipes that are easy to follow, simple to prepare, and most importantly, DELICIOUS.

In my opinion, a cookbook should be practical—not an autobiography. This book is purely dedicated to capturing the very essence of what a cookbook should be. But don't worry about it—it won't be too serious. Buckle up for another dose of my lighthearted humor, because that hasn't gone anywhere. We're going to cook good food and laugh along the way.

INTRODUCTION

After my first book, *Simply Korean*, came out, I was deeply touched by the incredible love and support I received—just saying "thank you" to my supporters hardly feels sufficient. Thanks to the enthusiasm and love, I've been blessed with the opportunity to reconnect with you through my second cookbook. I'd like to sincerely express my gratitude to anyone who appreciated my first book. Of course, I'd also like to warmly welcome and thank those who are encountering my recipes for the first time through this book.

One question I received after releasing my debut cookbook was *Why aren't more recipes that I enjoyed on your YouTube channel in this book?* The reason, briefly put, is that *Simply Korean* focused specifically on authentic Korean recipes anyone could make at any skill level. As a result, recipes that didn't fit neatly into Korean cuisine couldn't be included.

So now, with this book, I'm thrilled to share the 100 most popular recipes over the years. I genuinely wish I could offer you 300, 400, or even more recipes, but unfortunately, due to the physical limitations of a printed book, 100 is the maximum I could realistically include. I apologize in advance for this limitation. I guess you'll have to come back for my third and fourth books as well!

However, if you have both *Simply Korean* and *Beyond Korean*, I confidently assure you that you'll be able to enjoy nearly all your favorite East Asian dishes at home.
One last thing: I don't want this book to become a cool-looking encyclopedia or autobiography. Instead, my goal is to offer a practical, user-friendly cookbook filled with recipes you'll genuinely enjoy every day. At this point, some of you might start thinking, *Okay, it's simple, easy, and practical—I get it. But does that mean it's not as tasty?* Don't worry about it! As always, each recipe will deliver exceptional flavor. I guarantee it. Or your trusted taste tester, Claire, will guarantee it!

BEFORE WE GET STARTED...

I haven't categorized the recipes in this book too strictly. Instead, I simply divided them into four broad sections: Korean, Korean Fusion, Japanese, and Chinese cuisines. The reason I didn't categorize the recipes by protein is that in all the recipes in this book you can easily substitute proteins based on your preferences. While each recipe features a recommended protein, feel free to experiment, customize, and play around with it however you like. Trust me—they'll all taste amazing, just as always.

CLAIRE SAYS

Anyone who watches my YouTube channel will recognize my wife and taste tester, Claire. While she has always been my biggest fan, she's not afraid to be my biggest critic too. She is the first one to try every dish I make and provide her honest feedback—and that's no different here. Just like she did for my first book, Claire has approved every recipe in these pages. She even offers her own spin and perspective on my guidance (and might not always agree with me). Trust her; she knows what she's doing.

ESSENTIAL INGREDIENTS FOR BEYOND KOREAN

Asian cooking is essentially the art of chemistry, created through the combination of various sauces, seasonings, and condiments. Because of this, it often requires a wide range of ingredients, which can feel overwhelming for many people who are just starting out. But don't worry about it! Most of the recipes in this book are designed to be made with just fourteen essential ingredients, which I introduce here. Just like building blocks, you can combine these ingredients and easily create the 100 dishes featured in this book at home. Trust me. Once you stock up on these pantry essentials, you will be able to make amazing Asian dishes anytime. So go ahead and get them!

P.S. Since salt, black (or white) pepper, and vinegar are essential pantry items everywhere, I did not include them on this list.

1. **Soy Sauce**

   There are countless types of soy sauce in the world, each tailored to a specific purpose. While it's ideal to use the right soy sauce for each dish, our pantry space is limited. Therefore, I won't list them all here.

   In this book, when I mention "soy sauce," I am generally referring to products that are commonly labeled as light soy sauce, regular soy sauce, or all-purpose soy sauce. These varieties typically have a thin, clear consistency and are well-suited for use in stir-fries, soups, stews, dressings, and most other dishes.

   While soy sauces from Korea, Japan, and China are tailored to complement their respective cuisines, the differences among them are not too dramatic. Therefore, feel free to choose one that suits your taste—it will work just fine. Personally, I recommend using a 100% naturally brewed soy sauce that is rich in umami for the best flavor.

2. **Dark Soy Sauce**

   Commonly used in Chinese cuisine, dark soy sauce is thicker and darker than regular soy sauce. It is used to enhance the flavor of dishes and, more significantly, to provide a rich, dark color.

3. **Korean Fermented Chili Paste**
(Gochujang)
Gochujang is one of the most popular condiments in Korean cuisine. It adds not only a pleasant spiciness to dishes, but also a hint of sweetness and depth of flavor. Once opened, it is recommended to store in the fridge.

4. **Korean Fermented Soybean Paste**
(Doenjang)
Doenjang may not be as well-known as gochujang, but I believe it is the top condiment in Korean cuisine because it is truly an umami explosion with a sharp, salty, and deeply savory flavor. While it is primarily used in soups and stews, its umami richness also makes it suitable for use as a dipping sauce, dressing, or marinade. Once opened, it is recommended to store in the fridge.

5. **Chinese Chili Bean Paste**
(Doubanjiang)
Doubanjiang is a traditional Chinese fermented bean paste known for its spicy and salty flavor, which adds richness and depth to various spicy dishes. It is commonly used in Sichuan cuisine and recipes inspired by the bold flavors of this region. Once opened, it is recommended to store in the fridge.

6. **Korean Chili Pepper Flakes**
(Gochugaru)
A lot of people think all spicy Korean food is made using Korean chili paste (gochujang), but that is not true. In most cases (I'd say even 9 out of 10), dried chili pepper flakes are the real hero. They're not just for Korean dishes; they bring the perfect level of spiciness to enhance dishes from any cuisine.

7. Granulated Sugar

In Asian cuisine, sugar is not just a sweetener. It acts more as a flavor enhancer, so don't be afraid of using it. However, depending on your situation, the amount you include can be adjusted to your preference.

8. Oyster Sauce

This slightly sweet, salty, and incredibly flavorful sauce can elevate any dish—literally anything. That's why I sometimes even make pasta dishes with oyster sauce. A few pages later, in the Korean fusion section, you'll see how it works. (Sorry, Italians ... but trust me, once you try it, you'll understand why I do it. It's just too delicious. Love you!)

9. Korean Beef Stock Powder (Dasida)

This beef-flavored powder is designed to be mixed with water to make stock, but it can do so much more. When used as a seasoning, it acts like salt, soy sauce, doenjang, or gochujang, amplifying all the flavors. If your food is almost done cooking, but you still feel like something is missing, this magical seasoning powder will solve the problem. Dasida is available in many flavors (beef, seafood, clam, anchovy, etc.), but the recipes in this book only call for the beef flavor.

10. Chicken Bouillon Powder

Like oyster sauce, bouillon powder delivers super-concentrated, savory flavor. It's a perfect option for amping up the umami in dishes that need more depth.

11. Japanese Bonito Soup Stock Powder (Hondashi)

Dashi is a soup stock commonly used in Japanese cuisine, made from dried bonito flakes (katsuobushi) and kelp (kombu). This soup stock powder allows you to quickly and easily prepare a flavorful broth for Japanese soups and other dishes, enhancing them with a rich umami flavor.

12. Toasted Sesame Oil

Since it has a strong nutty flavor and aroma, toasted sesame oil is added in the last stage of cooking as a final touch in most Asian cuisines.

13. Fish Sauce

Fish sauce has a salty, savory, and pungent flavor. Some people may be concerned about using it because it sounds too fishy, but when used correctly, it won't make your food taste fishy at all. Instead, it adds a unique umami flavor that you may have never encountered before. Among the many varieties, I prefer the one made from anchovies.

14. Cooking Wine

This helps tenderize meat, eliminates any gamey or fishy taste, and works as an excellent flavor enhancer. There are many amazing cooking wines around the world, but most of the recipes in this book call for mirin, Shaoxing wine, or sake. However, that does not mean these three cooking wines are perfect substitutes for one another. You can certainly substitute ingredients, but be aware that doing so may change the authenticity of the dish. For instance, using Shaoxing wine as a substitute for mirin in Korean or Japanese dishes will bring a more Chinese-style aroma. Conversely, if you replace Shaoxing wine with mirin or sake in Chinese recipes, you may lose the distinctive flavor that is characteristic of Chinese cuisine.

A FEW NOTES FROM AARON

Measurements and Conversions

The recipes in this book use U.S. cup, tablespoon, and teaspoon measures. If you prefer metric measurements, please refer to the following conversions.

For ingredients measured by volume

Ingredient	Amount	Volume
Liquids (water, broth, soy sauce, oils, etc.)	1 cup	240 milliliters
	1 tablespoon	15 milliliters
	1 teaspoon	5 milliliters

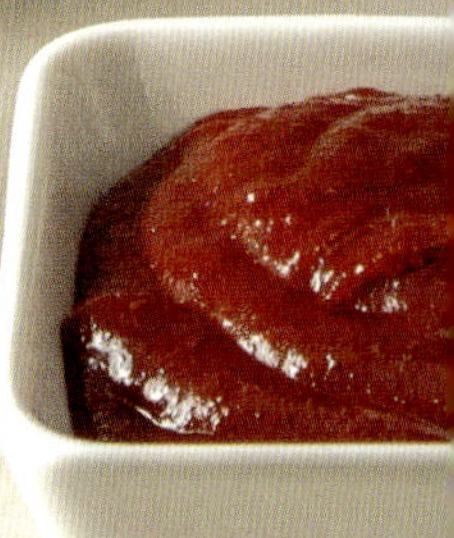

For ingredients measured by weight

Ingredient	Amount	Weight
All-Purpose Flour	1 cup 1 tablespoon	120 grams 7.5 grams
Cornstarch	1 cup 1 tablespoon	120 grams 7.5 grams
Potato Starch	1 cup 1 tablespoon	160 grams 10 grams
Granulated Sugar	1 cup 1 tablespoon	200 grams 12.5 grams
Salt	1 teaspoon	7 grams

KOREAN

CLAIRE SAYS:

Doenjang guk works great with literally any dish on Earth. And It comes in various delicious versions. Aaron shows you the classic spinach option, but feel free to use napa cabbage or bok choy for a tasty twist. Each ingredient brings its unique flavor, and everything will taste amazing.

SIGEUMCHI DOENJANG GUK

Korean Soybean Paste Soup with Spinach

PREP TIME: **10 minutes** // COOK TIME: **25 minutes** // SERVES: **5–6**

Claire always asks me to cook this soup when she's feeling under the weather. She says that, with a warm bowl of rice alongside it, this comforting, savory, and nourishing soup is like a cure-all. Whether it actually heals colds, I may never know, but this soup, which warms both body and soul, has become a beloved family tradition. Welcome to our family!

---

6 cups water or rice water
5 tbsp Korean soybean paste (doenjang)
½ tbsp Korean chili paste (gochujang)
1 tbsp Korean chili pepper flakes (gochugaru)
3 garlic cloves, finely chopped
½ tbsp Korean beef stock powder (Dasida)
7 oz (200g) spinach, trimmed and thoroughly washed
¼ large yellow onion, thinly sliced
2 green onions, thinly sliced
½ green chili pepper (optional), thinly sliced
½ mild red chili pepper (optional), thinly sliced
4½ oz (130g) medium-firm tofu, cut into ½-inch (1.25cm) cubes

1. Fill a pot with the water (or rice water). Add the Korean soybean paste and stir until it's dissolved. Bring to a boil. (If you dissolve Korean soybean paste with a strainer, it will be much easier and faster. And if you want cleaner soup, you can discard the solids.)
2. Once it begins to bubble, add the Korean chili paste, Korean chili pepper flakes, chopped garlic, Korean beef stock powder, spinach, onion, green onions, chili peppers (if using), and tofu. Simmer for 7 to 8 minutes over medium heat.
3. Transfer to a serving bowl. Serve with hot rice, kimchi, and your favorite banchan (small Korean side dishes).

NOTE: If the soup tastes a little bland to you, season it with more soybean paste. Don't use soy sauce or other seasonings.

OI MUCHIM

Spicy Cucumber Salad

PREP TIME: **10 minutes** // COOK TIME: **None** // SERVES: **2**

No matter when I eat it or what I pair it with, I could eat this Korean-style cucumber salad every single day for every meal. That's all I need to say.

---

1 English cucumber, thinly sliced

FOR THE SALAD DRESSING

1 tbsp Korean chili pepper flakes (gochugaru)

1½ tbsp white vinegar

1 tbsp granulated sugar

1 tbsp toasted sesame oil

½ tbsp toasted sesame seeds

½ tbsp minced garlic

½ tsp kosher salt, plus more if needed *(If you use fish sauce instead of kosher salt, you will get a deeper flavor.)*

1. In a medium bowl, whisk together all the salad dressing ingredients until thoroughly combined. Add the cucumber and toss together until coated well.
2. Taste and add more salt if needed. Enjoy!

CLAIRE SAYS:

Unlike kimchi, muchim (Korean-style salad) is best prepared in portions that can be consumed all at once. Over time, cucumbers release moisture and lose their crunch, which diminishes the fresh taste.

CLAIRE SAYS:

The best part of this dish is definitely the sauce. It's garlicky, salty, savory, and nutty with a hint of spiciness. So you can use this sauce with other vegetables such as grilled zucchini, steamed broccoli, etc. You will absolutely love it. You're welcome!

GAJI NAMUL

Spicy Garlic Eggplant

PREP TIME: **10 minutes** // COOK TIME: **5 minutes** // SERVES: **4**

This is a bit difficult to say, but I hated eggplant (back when I was a kid, of course). However, there was a moment that made me fall in love with them. Instead of the weird, slimy texture I used to dislike, it had a bouncy, yet soft and tender texture. And when the savory, garlicky, and slightly spicy eggplant met the warm rice, I actually felt guilty for all those years I avoided it. Yes, this Korean-style eggplant was a revolution for me. And it might be for you too.

---

1 lb (450g) eggplant, halved lengthwise and cut into 2-inch (5cm) chunks

Toasted sesame seeds, to garnish

FOR THE SPICY GARLIC SAUCE

3 garlic cloves, finely chopped

1–2 green onions, thinly sliced

½ mild red chili pepper (or bell pepper), thinly sliced

½ tbsp toasted sesame seeds, slightly crushed

1 tbsp soy sauce

½ tbsp granulated sugar

½ tbsp Korean chili pepper flakes (gochugaru)

1 tbsp fish sauce

½ tbsp toasted sesame oil

Freshly cracked black pepper, to taste

1. To prepare the spicy garlic sauce, in a small bowl, whisk together all the sauce ingredients until thoroughly combined. Set aside.
2. Set up a big pot with water and a steamer basket. Bring the water to a boil. Once it's boiling, carefully add the eggplant chunks. Cover and steam for 3 minutes, or until they have reached your desired doneness. (If you prefer a softer and creamier texture, steam for 5 minutes.) Remove the eggplant from the pot and set aside to cool.
3. When the eggplant is cool enough to handle, tear each chunk into bite-sized pieces with your hands.
4. In a large bowl, add the shredded eggplant and sauce. Gently toss together until the eggplant is beautifully coated. Sprinkle with sesame seeds and give a final mix. Serve with hot rice and other dishes, or store in an airtight container in the fridge for up to 3 days.

ALGAMJA JORIM

Braised Baby Potatoes

PREP TIME: **10 minutes** // COOK TIME: **35 minutes** // SERVES: **4**

This is one of the most beloved side dishes that you will always find on the table when you visit Korean restaurants. Yeah, those nice and fluffy baby potatoes coated in a sweet and savory glaze are truly the ultimate bite. They're so enjoyable that sometimes you might not even remember what the main dish was.

---

1 lb (450g) skin-on baby potatoes, cleaned
1½ tbsp neutral-tasting oil
2 garlic cloves, finely chopped
½ tsp dark soy sauce (optional), for color
2 tbsp honey (or rice syrup, light corn syrup, maple syrup)
1 tbsp toasted sesame oil (or perilla oil)
½ green chili pepper (optional), thinly sliced
½ mild red chili pepper (optional), thinly sliced
2 green onions, thinly sliced
Toasted sesame seeds, to garnish

FOR THE BRAISING SAUCE

½ cup water
4 tbsp soy sauce
2 tbsp mirin
1 tbsp granulated sugar
Freshly cracked black pepper, to taste
1 tbsp Korean chili pepper flakes (gochugaru) (optional)

1. Boil the potatoes for 15 minutes or until soft and easily pierced with a fork. Drain and let dry for 2 to 3 minutes or until the skins are no longer wet.
2. While the potatoes are cooking, make the braising sauce. In a small bowl, stir together all ingredients until fully incorporated. If you want some extra heat, you can add the tablespoon of Korean chili pepper flakes (gochugaru).
3. In a large wok or pan, heat the oil over medium heat. Once it gets hot, add the potatoes. Stir and cook for 3 to 5 minutes or until the potatoes get wrinkles on their skins and become golden brown.
4. Add the garlic and sauté for 30 seconds or until fragrant. Add the braising sauce and dark soy sauce (if using). Simmer for 8 minutes or until the sauce has reduced and thickened. Make sure to stir frequently for even coating.
5. Reduce the heat to low. Add the honey and stir to coat. Turn the heat off, add the sesame oil, and mix thoroughly. Add the chili peppers (if using) and green onions. Give a final mix.
6. Transfer to a serving plate and garnish with sesame seeds. Serve with hot rice and other dishes, or transfer to an airtight container and refrigerate for up to 3 days.

CLAIRE SAYS:

If you've only ever had these braised potatoes at restaurants, you haven't yet experienced their true potential. The real magic is revealed when it's freshly cooked and served straight from the pan. That's the kind of privilege you can only get by making it at home. So please give it a try—you'll find it tastes ten times better than anything you've ever tasted at a restaurant.

CLAIRE SAYS:

I'm sure you already know this, but I have to mention it. The best way to enjoy this green onion salad is to pair it with any meat. Trust me, it will enhance the flavor significantly.

PA MUCHIM

Green Onion Salad

PREP TIME: **10 minutes** // COOK TIME: **None** // SERVES: **4**

I've never seen anyone not ask for a refill of green onion salad at a Korean BBQ. People always get a mountain of this and finish with an empty plate. What? That's your story? Don't worry about it. I'm not spying on you... at least, not yet.

---

5 green onions (90g), cut into 4-inch (10cm) pieces and thinly sliced lengthwise *(To reduce the strong flavor, soak in cold water for 5 minutes and drain well.)*

FOR THE SALAD DRESSING

1 tbsp Korean chili pepper flakes (gochugaru)
1½ tbsp white vinegar
1 tbsp granulated sugar
1 tbsp toasted sesame oil
½ tbsp toasted sesame seeds
½ tbsp minced garlic
1 tsp fish sauce

1. In a small bowl, whisk together all the salad dressing ingredients until thoroughly combined. Add the green onions and toss until thoroughly coated. Please don't treat this like your laundry. Gently toss as if you're untangling the green onions.
2. Taste and add more salt or fish sauce to taste, if needed. Serve with Korean BBQ or any grilled meat dishes. Enjoy!

YANGBAECHU KIMCHI

Green Cabbage Kimchi

PREP TIME: **50 minutes** // COOK TIME: **None** // SERVES: **12**

As you already know, kimchi is one of the greatest vegetable dishes of all time. I shared the best traditional napa cabbage kimchi recipe in my previous cookbook, *Simply Korean*. But I understand not everyone has easy access to napa cabbage, so I made this kimchi recipe with green cabbage instead. It's easy to make, budget-friendly, and absolutely delicious. Trust me. Once you try it, you'll want to keep it in stock every month.

2.2 lb (1kg) green cabbage
½ cup coarse sea salt
4 cups water
4 oz (110g) green onions, cut into 2-inch (5cm) pieces
1 tbsp toasted sesame seeds

FOR THE KIMCHI PASTE

½ red apple, peeled and cut into small pieces
¼ yellow onion, peeled and cut into small pieces
5 garlic cloves
⅛ oz (4g) fresh ginger, peeled and thinly sliced
2 tbsp leftover cooked white rice
3 tbsp water
½ cup Korean chili pepper flakes (gochugaru)
1 tbsp granulated sugar
4 tbsp fish sauce

1. Discard a few outer layers of the cabbage. Cut out the core and chop into bite-sized pieces. Separate the cabbage layers and transfer them to a large bowl. (Make sure the leaves are not stuck together. They won't get salted evenly.)
2. Sprinkle the salt over the cabbage and toss until evenly coated. Pour the water in and toss to combine. Let sit for 30 minutes. Mix occasionally so that they are evenly salted.
3. Once the cabbage becomes flexible, rinse thoroughly under cold water at least 3 times. Drain well and gently squeeze to get rid of excess water. The cabbage should be a little salty, but not extremely so. Set aside.
4. To make the kimchi paste, to a blender, add the apple, yellow onion, garlic, ginger, cold rice, and water. Blend on high until smooth.
5. To a medium bowl, add the apple mixture, the Korean chili pepper flakes, sugar, and fish sauce, and stir together until thoroughly combined.
6. Transfer the cabbage to a clean large bowl. (If you are reusing the same bowl from earlier, make sure it's been washed to remove any leftover salt.) Add the green onions, sesame seeds and kimchi paste, and mix together with gloved hands until thoroughly coated. Taste and add more salt or fish sauce if needed.
7. Transfer to a large, lidded container. Press down on the cabbage kimchi so there are no air pockets, and seal with a lid. Let sit at room temperature for 5 to 6 hours. Then refrigerate. Once it's cold, green cabbage kimchi is ready to serve and will last in the fridge for about 1 month. (Green cabbage kimchi can be enjoyed immediately without fermentation, like geotjeori kimchi [fresh kimchi], so it can be served right away.)

CLAIRE SAYS:

Just like traditional kimchi, this green cabbage kimchi is also spicy, garlicky, and packed with umami, but it's much crunchier and more refreshing than other kimchi and that is the beauty of it. For that reason, it will not only work great with Korean dishes but also with almost every dish around the world. Trust me. You can enjoy this with just about anything.

CLAIRE SAYS:

When you crave a lighter and more refreshing kimchi, this is the way to go. Unlike regular kimchi, it doesn't require fermentation or even salting, so you can casually enjoy it like a salad.

TOMATO KIMCHI

Tomato Kimchi

PREP TIME: **20 minutes** // COOK TIME: **None** // MAKES: **8**

As a Korean, I have spent my whole life tasting millions of different kimchi. And as a former Korean chef, I also spent my entire life learning how to make kimchi more delicious. So I think I can confidently say that this is one of the easiest kimchis of all time. Trust me. This is not the most traditional kimchi, but I dare say it will be the simplest and most delicious kimchi you will ever make. I guarantee it.

½ yellow onion, thinly sliced *(To reduce the strong onion flavor, soak in cold water for 5 minutes and thoroughly pat dry.)*
4 oz (115g) garlic chives, cut into 2-inch (5cm) pieces
⅓ carrot (60g), cut into thin matchsticks
8 ripe tomatoes, cores removed and cut into wedges

FOR THE TOMATO KIMCHI PASTE

5 tbsp Korean chili pepper flakes (gochugaru)
4 tbsp fish sauce *(Saltiness varies by brand. Add more or less if needed.)*
1½ tbsp granulated sugar
1 tbsp honey
1 tbsp toasted sesame seeds
4 garlic cloves, finely chopped
1 tsp freshly grated ginger

1. To prepare the tomato kimchi paste, in a small bowl, stir together all the ingredients until thoroughly combined. (You can reduce the amount of chili pepper flakes to make it less spicy.)
2. To a large bowl, add the kimchi paste, onion, garlic chives, and carrot. Gently toss together with gloved hands so that they don't get mushy.
3. Add the tomatoes. With gloved hands, gently toss everything together, making sure every piece of the tomato is thoroughly coated. Taste and add more fish sauce, if needed.
4. Transfer to a serving plate and serve with hot rice, Korean BBQ, or other side dishes, or store in an airtight container in the fridge for up to a week.

NOTES: This kimchi should not be used to make other dishes such as kimchi fried rice and kimchi soft tofu stew. It is not that kind of kimchi. Just enjoy it by itself like a salad. It's so delicious just the way it is that you won't even think of other dishes.

As the days pass, the tomatoes will release some juice, but that's totally normal. Just be sure to drizzle a few scoops of that juice over the tomatoes when serving.

OI KIMCHI

Cucumber Kimchi

PREP TIME: **50 minutes** // COOK TIME: **None** // SERVES: **20**

I know making kimchi might sound intimidating. You might think you need a bunch of special ingredients and can't even begin. But don't worry about it. Not all kimchi has to be that complicated. Trust me, as long as you have some cucumbers, you're already on your way to making one of the best kimchis you've ever tasted.

---

10 English cucumbers, about 4½ lb (2kg) in total, rinsed

2 tbsp coarse sea salt (or 1 tbsp kosher salt)

7 green onions (105g), cut into 2-inch (5cm) pieces

FOR THE CUCUMBER KIMCHI PASTE

5 tbsp Korean chili pepper flakes (gochugaru)

5 tbsp fish sauce, plus more to taste *(Saltiness varies by brand. Add more or less as needed.)*

1½ tbsp granulated sugar

6 garlic cloves, finely chopped

1 tsp freshly grated ginger

1. Trim off both ends of the cucumbers and cut them in half lengthwise. Using a spoon, scrape out the watery seeds. Cut each cucumber in half again lengthwise, then cut them into 2-inch (5cm) pieces. Transfer to a large mixing bowl.
2. Sprinkle the salt over the cucumber pieces. Gently toss together so that the cucumbers get salted evenly. Let sit for 10 minutes. (This salting process will draw out the moisture, so the cucumbers will become nice and crunchy.)
3. Place the cucumbers in a colander and let drain for 20 minutes. Rinse them in cold water a few times and drain well. (Grab a piece and taste. If it's too salty, please give them another rinse.)
4. To make the cucumber kimchi paste, in a medium bowl, combine all the ingredients until thoroughly mixed.
5. To a large bowl, add the salted cucumbers and the kimchi paste. With gloved hands, gently toss together until every piece of the cucumber is thoroughly coated. Add the green onions and give everything another gentle toss. Give it a quick taste. If you want it to be saltier, add a little bit more fish sauce.
6. Transfer to an airtight container. To promote the fermentation process, let sit at room temperature for 3 to 4 hours and store in the fridge after. Once it's chilled, this cucumber kimchi is ready to serve. Keep for up to 2 to 3 weeks in the fridge.

NOTE: As the cucumber kimchi ferments, you will see some liquid in the container—this is totally normal.

CLAIRE SAYS:
This spicy, salty, and refreshing cucumber kimchi goes perfectly well with any meal. But my picks are the Dakgogi Bibimbap (page 44) and Avocado Gyeranbap (page 43).

CLAIRE SAYS:

If you are a big fan of Korean seasoned seaweed (gim), you can add some. It will add a nice layer of savoriness and umami to your gyeranbap.

AVOCADO GYERANBAP

Egg Rice Bowl with Avocado

PREP TIME: **5 minutes** // COOK TIME: **5 minutes** // SERVES: **1**

Korean egg rice, known as gyeranbap, has become hugely popular as the simplest yet most delicious rice bowl. This humble combination of rice, a fried egg, soy sauce, and a hint of sesame oil shows the beauty of simplicity. Now, with the addition of creamy avocado, this rice bowl is sure to be remembered as one of the greatest dishes in rice bowl history.

---

1 tbsp neutral-tasting oil
1–2 large egg(s)
1 cup hot cooked short-grain white rice, about 7½ oz (210g)
½ avocado, thinly sliced
1 tsp soy sauce, plus more to taste
1 tsp toasted sesame oil (or unsalted butter)
½ green onion (optional), thinly sliced
Generous pinch of toasted sesame seeds, to garnish

1. In a medium skillet, heat the oil over medium-low heat until hot. Carefully crack the egg(s) into the pan and cook to your desired doneness. (I recommend sunny-side up eggs because the runny egg yolk will become a part of the sauce.)
2. Place the rice in a serving bowl and top with the egg(s) and avocado. Finish off with the soy sauce, sesame oil, green onion (if using), and sesame seeds. Enjoy with kimchi or Oi Muchim (page 28).

DAKGOGI BIBIMBAP

Mixed Rice with Vegetables and Chicken

PREP TIME: **20 minutes** // COOK TIME: **10 minutes** // SERVES: **2**

A bowl of hot rice, some meat and veggies, and there's even a sauce that brings the whole thing together. Bibimbap has everything you would want in your meal, right? But traditional bibimbap might seem complicated since you have to cook every single vegetable separately. But don't worry about it. This chicken bibimbap only needs some fresh vegetables. So, when you're not in the mood to stand over a hot stove, this bad boy will come to your mind.

- ½ tbsp neutral-tasting oil, plus more for fried eggs
- 10½ oz (300g) boneless chicken thighs, cut into bite-sized pieces
- 2 cups hot cooked short-grain white rice, about 7½ oz (210g) for each serving
- 2 tbsp toasted sesame oil, divided
- ¼ yellow onion, thinly sliced *(To reduce the strong onion flavor, soak it in cold water for 5 minutes and thoroughly pat dry.)*
- 2 lettuce leaves, cut into thin strips
- 2 green cabbage leaves, thinly sliced
- 4 perilla leaves (optional), thinly sliced
- ⅓ carrot (60g), julienned
- ½ English cucumber, julienned
- 2 fried eggs, to serve
- Generous pinch of toasted sesame seeds, to garnish

FOR THE GOCHUJANG-BASED BIBIMBAP SAUCE (SPICY VERSION)

- 4 tbsp Korean chili paste (gochujang)
- 2 tbsp granulated sugar
- 1 tbsp white vinegar
- 1 tbsp lemon juice
- 1 tsp minced garlic
- ½ tbsp toasted sesame seeds
- 2 tbsp lemon-lime soda, such as Sprite

FOR THE SOY SAUCE–BASED BIBIMBAP SAUCE (NON-SPICY VERSION)

- 4 tbsp soy sauce
- ½ tbsp granulated sugar
- 1 tbsp mirin (optional)
- 1 tbsp sliced green onion
- 1 mild red chili pepper (optional), finely chopped
- 1 tsp minced garlic
- ½ tbsp toasted sesame seeds

FOR THE CHICKEN TOPPING SAUCE

- 1 tbsp soy sauce
- 1 tbsp mirin
- 1 tsp granulated sugar
- 1 tbsp minced garlic
- ½ tbsp toasted sesame oil
- Freshly cracked black pepper, to taste

1. To make the bibimbap sauce (gochujang- or soy sauce–based), in a small bowl, stir together all ingredients until fully incorporated. Use immediately or store in an airtight container in the fridge for up to 1 week. (If this sounds like too much work for you, you can just use some gochujang straight from the container.)
2. To make the chicken topping sauce, in a small bowl, stir together all the ingredients until fully incorporated. Set aside.
3. In a large skillet or pan, heat the oil over medium-high heat. Once it gets nice and hot, add the chicken pieces in a single layer. Sear for 2 to 3 minutes or until nicely browned on the bottom. Flip and cook the other side for another 2 minutes or until cooked through.
4. Pour in the chicken topping sauce. Toss together for 1 minute or until they are nicely coated. Remove from the pan and set aside.
5. To serve, divide the rice evenly between two bowls. Drizzle with the sesame oil. Evenly distribute the vegetables and chicken. Place the fried eggs on top and sprinkle with sesame seeds. Serve with your preferred bibimbap sauce. Enjoy!

CLAIRE SAYS:

The amount of bibimbap sauce you need is not fixed. The best way to enjoy bibimbap is to add the sauce gradually and adjust it to your taste. Start with 1 tablespoon, mix everything thoroughly, and add more sauce until you find the perfect ratio. This will be the fun part of eating bibimbap.

CLAIRE SAYS:

Perilla oil goes really well with balsamic vinegar, so sometimes Aaron makes this noodle dish with balsamic vinegar. If you want to give it a little bit of a twist, please use some. It will taste fancier, and you will be surprised.

DEULGIREUM MAKGUKSU

Perilla Oil Noodles

PREP TIME: **10 minutes** // COOK TIME: **10 minutes** // SERVES: **2**

This noodle dish represents beauty in simplicity. The incredible aroma of perilla oil and the flavorful soy sauce create an amazing flavor. And that simple symphony makes this dish the King of Korean noodle dishes. Seriously, if you are a big fan of pasta salad, you can't say no to this.

---

2 sheets unseasoned dried seaweed (dried seaweed for gimbap or sushi), torn into smaller pieces
4 tbsp toasted sesame seeds
7 oz (200g) dried buckwheat noodles (or soba noodles)
Microgreens (or thinly sliced lettuce), to garnish
1 soft or hard-boiled egg (optional), to serve
2 green onions, thinly sliced

FOR THE SAUCE

3½ tbsp soy sauce, plus more if needed
1 tbsp granulated sugar
1 tbsp white vinegar
4 tbsp perilla oil

1. To a blender, add the dried seaweed pieces, along with the sesame seeds. Blend on high until they become a fine powder. (If you are using seasoned dried seaweed, grind the sesame seeds with a mortar and pestle and just tear the seaweed with your hands and add the pieces at the end.) Set aside.
2. To make the sauce, in a large bowl, stir together all the ingredients until thoroughly combined. Set aside.
3. Cook the noodles in a pot of water according to the package instructions. (If the water rises up and it's about to boil over, add half a cup of water. Repeat two or three times until the noodles are cooked through.) Rinse the cooked noodles well under cold water. This will help remove some of the starch and make the noodles more chewy and bouncy.
4. Squeeze out the noodles as best as you can. Let them drain for 1 or 2 minutes.
5. Add the drained noodles to the bowl with the sauce and mix by hand until thoroughly combined. Taste and add more soy sauce if needed.
6. Divide the noodles evenly between two serving bowls. Top with the seaweed and sesame seed mixture, microgreens, and boiled egg (if using). Sprinkle with green onions. Enjoy!

NOTES: If you can't find dried buckwheat noodles or soba noodles, substitute spaghetti noodles. They will work great in this recipe.

If you can't find perilla oil, substitute 3 tablespoons of toasted sesame oil. While it tastes different, it will still be fantastic!

GANJANG BIBIM GUKSU

Korean Soy Sauce Noodles

PREP TIME: **10 minutes** // COOK TIME: **10 minutes** // SERVES: **2**

If you're not a big fan of spicy food and can't handle the heat of spicy bibim guksu, which is one of the best Korean noodle dishes, then this is the way to go. This dish offers a perfect balance of savoriness, umami, beefy flavor, and a slightly sweet yet salty sauce. Trust me, these mixed noodles have everything you'd want in a noodle dish.

½ tbsp neutral-tasting oil
7 oz (200g) ground beef
7 oz (200g) somyeon noodles (Korean dried wheat noodles)
½ English cucumber, julienned
2 green onions, thinly sliced
1 soft or hard-boiled egg (optional), to serve
2 tbsp toasted sesame seeds, ground

FOR THE BEEF TOPPING SAUCE

1 tbsp soy sauce
½ tbsp oyster sauce
½ tbsp mirin
1 tsp granulated sugar
2 garlic cloves, finely chopped
½ tbsp toasted sesame oil
Black pepper, to taste

FOR THE NOODLE SAUCE

3 tbsp soy sauce
2 tbsp white vinegar
1 tbsp granulated sugar
1 tbsp light corn syrup (or honey)
2 tbsp toasted sesame oil
Black pepper, to taste
Small pinch of MSG (optional)

1. To make the beef topping sauce, in a small bowl, stir together all the ingredients until thoroughly combined. Set aside.
2. In a large wok or pan, heat the oil over medium-high heat. Once it gets nice and hot, add the ground beef. Spread it out and sear for 1 to 2 minutes or until nicely browned on the bottom. Flip and break up the beef. Stir-fry it for 2 minutes. When the beef is cooked, pour in the beef topping sauce and keep tossing it around for 1 to 2 minutes. Turn the heat off and set aside.
3. Cook the noodles in a pot of boiling water according to the package instructions. Rinse the cooked noodles well under cold water. Once cool, place the noodles in a bowl of cold water and "do the laundry" (rub them with both hands) to get rid of the starch on their surface. Rinse the noodles under cold water again. Drain and squeeze out any excess water from the noodles.
4. To make the noodle sauce, in a small bowl, stir together all the ingredients until fully incorporated.
5. In a large mixing bowl, add the drained noodles, beef, and noodle sauce. Mix by hand until thoroughly combined.
6. Divide the noodles evenly between two serving bowls. Top with the cucumber, green onions, and boiled egg (if using). Sprinkle on some ground sesame seeds.

CLAIRE SAYS:

You can use any protein you like instead of ground beef. Chicken, pork, or even tofu work really well with this recipe, so feel free to play around with it. Everything will be fantastic.

CLAIRE SAYS:

Aaron has described a very traditional and authentic way of serving, but you don't necessarily need to use a ttukbaegi (Korean earthenware pot). You can finish the dish in the same pot you cooked it in, or you can use any small, heavy-bottomed pot as an alternative, so there's no need to worry if you don't have a ttukbaegi.

KIMCHI SUNDUBU JJIGAE

Kimchi Soft Tofu Stew

PREP TIME: **15 minutes** // COOK TIME: **20 minutes** // SERVES: **3–4**

There are so many great food combos: bacon and eggs, burgers and fries, spaghetti and meatballs ... Among those amazing combos, let me introduce one of the best combinations in Korean cuisine: kimchi and soft tofu stew (sundubu jjigae).

2½ tbsp neutral-tasting oil
7 oz (200g) pork belly or pork shoulder, cut into bite-sized pieces
3 green onions, thinly sliced, white and green parts divided
3 garlic cloves, finely chopped
2 tbsp soju (or sake, water)
1 cup (200g) well-fermented kimchi, cut into bite-sized pieces (see note)
3 cups water or rice water (see note)
¼ tsp kosher salt, to season
2 (1½ lb/700g) packages silken tofu, halved
2 eggs, to serve
1 spicy green chili pepper (optional), thinly sliced
1 mild red chili pepper (optional), thinly sliced
Freshly cracked black pepper, to taste

FOR THE SEASONING PASTE

3 tbsp Korean chili pepper flakes (gochugaru)
1 tbsp soy sauce
1 tbsp fish sauce
½ tsp granulated sugar
1 tbsp Korean beef stock powder (Dasida) or chicken bouillon powder
½ tsp freshly cracked black pepper

1. To make the seasoning paste, in a small bowl, stir together all the ingredients until thoroughly combined. Set aside.
2. In a large wok or pot, add the oil and pork. Turn on the heat to medium-high and cook for 5 minutes or until most of the fat has rendered out and the pork is nicely browned on both sides.
3. Add the white parts of the green onions and the garlic. Sauté for 1 or 2 minutes or until they start to pick up some color. Add the soju and stir for 1 minute.
4. Reduce the heat to medium. Add the kimchi and the seasoning paste. Sauté for 4 to 5 minutes or until the kimchi is wilted down. (Chili pepper flakes burn easily, so make sure to keep stirring to prevent them from burning.)
5. Add the water and bring to a boil. Once bubbling away, reduce the heat to medium-high and simmer for 5 more minutes.
6. Add the salt and the silken tofu. Using a spoon, break the tofu into nice, big chunks. Simmer for 3 more minutes.
7. To serve, transfer the stew into a ttukbaegi (Korean earthenware pot), and place over medium-high heat. As soon as it begins to bubble, immediately crack the eggs on top of the stew, and cook to your desired doneness.
8. Finish off with the greens of the green onions, sliced chili peppers (if using), and a few cracks of black pepper to taste. Serve with a bowl of hot rice. Enjoy!

NOTE: Well-fermented kimchi is the key to this recipe, so if your kimchi is freshly made, please wait until it tastes a little bit sour.

When you cook rice, reserve the water from washing the rice. Rice water (ssalddeumul) can be used in place of water for Korean soups or stews. The starch from the rice water will help enhance the flavor.

TTEOKBOKKI

Classic Spicy Rice Cakes

PREP TIME: **5 minutes** // COOK TIME: **10 minutes** // SERVES: **3–4**

It's no exaggeration to say that this spicy, slightly sweet, and chewy tteokbokki almost dominates the world of street food. Due to its popularity, millions of different variations of tteokbokki have emerged. However, it's an unchanging truth that the classic version is the best.

---

3 cups water
½ tbsp Korean beef stock powder (Dasida) or chicken bouillon powder
1.3 lb (600g) Korean rice cakes (cylinder-shaped)
3 sheets Korean fish cakes, about 4 oz (120g) in total, cut into bite-sized pieces
3–4 green onions, cut into 2-inch (5cm) pieces
2 hard-boiled eggs

FOR THE SEASONING PASTE

2 tbsp Korean chili pepper flakes (gochugaru)
2 tbsp Korean chili paste (gochujang)
2 tbsp granulated sugar
3 tbsp light corn syrup
1 tbsp Korean beef stock powder (Dasida) or chicken bouillon powder
¼ tsp freshly cracked black pepper

1. To make the seasoning paste, in a small bowl, combine all the seasoning ingredients. Mix until thoroughly incorporated. Set aside.
2. In a medium bowl, combine the water with the Korean beef stock powder (or chicken bouillon powder). Set aside.
3. To a large pan, add the rice cakes, fish cakes, green onions, and hard-boiled eggs. Add in the seasoning paste and the stock. Bring to a boil.
4. Once it begins to bubble, reduce the heat to medium. Simmer, stirring occasionally, for 13 minutes or until the sauce is thickened and the rice cakes are soft and cooked through.
5. Transfer to a serving plate or serve directly from the pan. Enjoy!

NOTE: If using frozen rice cakes, thaw in the fridge overnight.

CLAIRE SAYS:

This old-school tteokbokki is the one Aaron and I grew up eating. Nothing fancy, but to me, this is the greatest tteokbokki of all time. That's all I want to say.

CHAMCHI GIMBAP

Seaweed Rice Rolls with Creamy Tuna

PREP TIME: **1 hour** // COOK TIME: **5 minutes** // SERVES: **5**

I'm a person who loves gimbap more than anyone. Ask Claire how many times I say "I want gimbap." Her answer would be three or four times a week. As the biggest fan of gimbap and someone who has tried it countless times, I can confidently say this tuna recipe deserves to be called the king of gimbaps. (Sorry, bulgogi gimbap—it was a close game.)

CLAIRE SAYS:

I feel like I'm experiencing déjà vu. Three years ago, I clearly remember commenting on the gimbap recipe that its true soulmate is tteokbokki. I thought about writing something different this time, but I think I have to say that again: the true soulmate of this tuna kimbap is also tteokbokki. So, when you eat this gimbap, make sure to pair it with the Tteokbokki (page 52). You'll understand why I emphasized it twice.

4 cups cooked short-grain white rice
1½ tbsp toasted sesame oil, plus more to coat rolls
½ tsp kosher salt
1 tsp toasted sesame seeds, plus more to garnish
6 dried seaweed sheets (gim or sushi nori)
12 perilla leaves, stems removed
6 imitation crab sticks or piece of crabmeat (optional)
6 pieces gimbap ham or sausage, lightly seared
6 strips Korean yellow pickled radish (danmuji) *(If you can't get precut danmuji, cut into 7-inch (18cm) strips.)*

FOR THE CREAMY TUNA SALAD FILLING

10 oz (280g) canned tuna, drained
4 tbsp Kewpie mayonnaise
Freshly cracked black pepper, to taste
2 tbsp green onion (optional), thinly sliced
½ green chili pepper (optional), finely chopped

FOR THE SPINACH FILLING

8 oz (230g) spinach, blanched, rinsed in cold water, and drained
½ tbsp minced garlic
¼ tsp kosher salt
1 tbsp toasted sesame oil
½ tbsp toasted sesame seeds

FOR THE CARROT FILLING

1 tbsp neutral-tasting oil
1 large carrot, julienned
Generous pinch of kosher salt

FOR THE OMELET FILLING

4 large eggs
Generous pinch of kosher salt
½ tbsp neutral-tasting oil

1. To prepare the creamy tuna salad filling, in a medium bowl, combine all the ingredients. Set aside.
2. To prepare the spinach filling, in a medium bowl, combine all the ingredients. Gently mix by hand and put it on a large platter.
3. To prepare the carrot filling, in a medium nonstick skillet or pan, heat the oil over medium heat. Once it gets nice and hot, add the carrot and salt, and sauté for 1 or 2 minutes or until the carrot is just beginning to soften. Transfer it to the platter next to the spinach.
4. To prepare the omelet filling, whisk together the eggs and salt. In a medium-large nonstick skillet or pan, drizzle the oil, swirl to coat the bottom, and wipe off the excess with a paper towel. Heat the pan over medium heat. Working in batches, pour a thin layer of the egg mixture and tilt the pan from side to side to spread out evenly. Once the bottom is cooked, flip over and cook until the eggs are fully cooked. Remove the omelet from the pan, fold it in half twice in one direction, and cut into thin strips. Put it on the platter next to the carrot.
5. To a large bowl, add the cooked rice, sesame oil, salt, and sesame seeds. Gently mix together with a spatula or wooden spoon.
6. Place a sheet of dried seaweed on a bamboo mat, shiny-side down and rough-side up. Place ¾ cup of seasoned rice on the sheet, and evenly spread to cover the bottom ¾ of the sheet with about 1.5 inches (3.5cm) left uncovered at the top. (Moisten your hands with water before grabbing the rice. Otherwise, your hands will be like hedgehogs made of steamed rice!)
7. Place two perilla leaves at the bottom third of the seaweed sheet. Place some tuna salad, egg omelet, carrot, spinach, a crab stick (if using), a piece of ham, and a Korean yellow pickled radish strip in an orderly row on the perilla leaves.
8. Place your thumbs under the bamboo mat, hold all the fillings with your other fingers, and lift the bottom. Roll it up from the bottom, making sure that the bottom edge of the rice touches the top edge of the rice to fully enclose the fillings. Continue rolling, holding the mat with both hands, and pressing tightly. Spread some water on the upper exposed portion of the seaweed, roll completely, and apply a light pressure to completely seal. Remove from the mat and place the gimbap seam-side down on a plate. Repeat with the rest of the ingredients.
9. Generously spread sesame oil onto the rolls, and slice into ½ to ¾-inch (1.25–2cm) rolls or bite-sized pieces. (Coating your knife with sesame oil will prevent the seasoned rice from sticking to it and help it cut more easily.) Finish off with some sesame seeds.

DAKGANGJEONG

Street-Style Korean Fried Chicken

PREP TIME: **15 minutes + 1 hour to brine** // COOK TIME: **20 minutes** // SERVES: **3**

Over the past half century, Korean fried chicken has experienced an incredible evolution. While I haven't counted them all, there are likely hundreds of variations out there. But, as always, trends tend to circle back to the classics. Once you try this classic Korean-style fried chicken, you'll understand why it has been a staple at street stalls, traditional markets, and even grocery stores for many years.

1.3 lb (600g) boneless, skinless chicken thighs (or breasts), cut into bite-sized pieces
1 cup all-purpose flour
1 cup potato starch (or cornstarch)
Kosher salt, to taste
1 cup cold water
High-heat oil (such as canola, avocado, vegetable, etc.), for frying
1 tbsp neutral-tasting oil
1 green onion (optional), thinly sliced, to garnish
⅛ cup roasted peanuts (optional), crushed, to garnish

FOR THE BRINE

½ tbsp kosher salt
1 tbsp granulated sugar
1 tbsp chicken bouillon powder
1 tbsp garlic powder
1 tbsp onion powder
½ tbsp cayenne pepper
1 tbsp white vinegar
½ tsp freshly cracked black pepper
3 cups water

FOR THE DAKGANGJEONG SAUCE

2 tbsp Korean chili paste (gochujang)
½ tbsp Korean chili pepper flakes (gochugaru)
1 tbsp soy sauce
½ tbsp oyster sauce
1 tbsp granulated sugar
6 tbsp light corn syrup
1 tbsp minced garlic
2 tbsp ketchup
1 tbsp mirin
3 tbsp water

1. To prepare the brine, in a large bowl, combine all the ingredients and stir until everything is fully dissolved.
2. Add the chicken to the brine, cover with a lid or plastic wrap, and refrigerate for at least 1 hour or overnight.
3. To make the dakgangjeong sauce, in a small bowl, combine all the ingredients. Mix until thoroughly combined. Set aside.
4. In a separate bowl, whisk together the flour, potato starch, and salt. To make a wet batter, transfer half of the mixture into another bowl, add 1 cup of cold water, and mix well until thoroughly combined.
5. Transfer the chicken pieces into the wet batter and then coat with the dry batter little by little. (To make it easier, transfer the dry batter to a wide tray and coat the chicken pieces in small batches.)
6. In a large Dutch oven or heavy-bottomed pot, heat about 2 inches (5cm) of cooking oil to 340°F (170°C). Working in batches, carefully place the chicken pieces in the oil. (The batter can be a bit sticky. Be careful when you add them in.) Fry for 4 minutes or until light brown. Remove from the hot oil and place on a wire rack. Repeat with the remaining chicken pieces.
7. Increase the oil temperature to 355°F (180°C). Fry the chicken pieces a second time for 3 minutes until golden brown and crispy. Transfer to the wire rack and rest.
8. In a large wok or pan, add the neutral-tasting oil and heat over medium heat. Once it gets nice and hot, add the dakgangjeong sauce and stir for 2 minutes or until bubbling. Add all the fried chicken and toss together for 2 minutes or until each piece is thoroughly coated and glossy.
9. Transfer to a serving plate and garnish with the green onion and peanuts (if using). Enjoy!

CLAIRE SAYS:
Compared to other Korean fried chicken varieties, the best thing about dakgangjeong is that it's made with boneless chicken. No need to get your hands messy and it's so convenient to eat, so I think it's perfect for potluck parties. The moment you bring this dish to the table, you're sure to become the superstar on that day.

CLAIRE SAYS:

As Aaron mentioned, these gochujang chicken wings are a great alternative to buffalo wings and a perfect option for those who are intimidated by deep-frying at home but still want to experience Korean fried chicken. The taste? Finger-licking good!

GOCHUJANG DAKNALGAE

Gochujang Chicken Wings

PREP TIME: **20 minutes** // COOK TIME: **20 minutes** // SERVES: **2**

Sure, sure, we all know that buffalo wings are great. But don't you get tired of eating the same wings every time? Don't you want something new with a Korean twist? If your answer is yes, our gochujang sauce full of umami will take you to a whole new world.

1.3 lb (600g) chicken wings
Kosher salt and black pepper, to taste
¼ cup cornstarch
3 tbsp neutral-tasting oil, plus more if needed
5 garlic cloves, finely chopped
2 green onions, thinly sliced, white and green parts divided
½ tsp freshly grated ginger
½ tsp toasted sesame seeds, to garnish

FOR THE SAUCE

2 tbsp Korean chili pepper flakes (gochugaru)
1 tbsp granulated sugar
2 tbsp Korean chili paste (gochujang)
1 tbsp soy sauce
1 tbsp oyster sauce
½ tbsp chicken bouillon powder
1 tbsp light corn syrup
2 tbsp mirin
¼ cup water

1. To make the sauce, in a small bowl, stir together all the ingredients until fully incorporated. Set aside.
2. Use a knife to make small cuts between the bones of the chicken wings. Pat dry with paper towels. Season the chicken wings with salt and pepper and lightly coat them with cornstarch. Make sure they are evenly coated and shake off the excess.
3. In a large pan, heat the oil over medium heat. Once it gets nice and hot, add the chicken wings and cook for 8 to 10 minutes or until they are golden brown and cooked through. Remove them from the pan and set aside.
4. To the same pan, add the garlic, the white parts of the green onions, and ginger. Sauté for 1 minute or until fragrant. Add more oil if the mixture is too dry.
5. Add the sauce mixture and bring it to a boil over high heat. Once the sauce comes to a boil, add the cooked chicken wings and toss together until the chicken is fully coated.
6. Transfer to a serving plate and finish with the sesame seeds and the green parts of the green onions. Enjoy!

GANJANG DAKNALGAE

Soy Sauce Chicken Wings

PREP TIME: **20 minutes** // COOK TIME: **20 minutes** // SERVES: **2**

I know all of you guys love my Korean fried chicken recipe, especially the one with honey soy sauce. Ultra crispy fried chicken smothered in a sweet and savory sauce—who wouldn't fall in love with it? However, the main hurdle is deep-frying. If the thought of deep-frying intimidates you, but you're still eager to try Korean-style fried chicken, trust me, this is the way to go.

1.3 lb (600g) chicken wings
Kosher salt and black pepper, to taste
¼ cup cornstarch
3 tbsp neutral-tasting oil, plus more if needed
5 garlic cloves, finely chopped
2 green onions, thinly sliced, white and green parts divided
½ tsp freshly grated ginger
10 shishito peppers (60g), cut into bite-sized pieces
½ tsp toasted sesame seeds, to garnish
1 mild red chili pepper (optional), thinly sliced, to garnish

FOR THE SAUCE

2½ tbsp soy sauce
1 tbsp honey
1 tbsp granulated sugar
2 tbsp oyster sauce
1 tbsp mirin
½ tbsp chicken bouillon powder
¼ cup water
1 Vietnamese dried chili (optional)

1. To make the sauce, in a small bowl, stir together all the ingredients until fully incorporated. Set aside.
2. Use a knife and make small cuts between the bones of the chicken wings. Pat dry with paper towels. Season the chicken wings with salt and pepper and lightly coat them with cornstarch. Make sure they are evenly coated and shake off the excess.
3. In a large pan, heat the oil over medium heat. Once it gets nice and hot, add the chicken wings and cook for 8 to 10 minutes or until they are golden brown and cooked through. Remove from the pan and set aside.
4. To the same pan, add the garlic, the white parts of the green onions, and ginger. Sauté for 1 minute or until fragrant. Add more oil if the mixture is too dry.
5. Add the sauce mixture and bring it to a boil over high heat. Once the sauce comes to a boil, add the cooked chicken wings and toss together until the chicken is fully coated. Add the shishito peppers and stir-fry for 30 seconds.
6. Transfer to a serving plate and finish with the sesame seeds, the green parts of the green onions, and red chili pepper (if using).

CLAIRE SAYS:

These sticky, savory, soy-glazed chicken wings are packed with incredible flavor and aroma. Perfect for parties, picnics, or even late-night snacks. And of course, it works great with drinks. You know what I mean ... if you're over 21!

CLAIRE SAYS:

If you have access to an outdoor charcoal grill, that's definitely the best way to enjoy this dwaeji galbi. The incredible smoky, charred flavor from the charcoal will truly amaze your taste buds.

DWAEJI GALBI

Korean BBQ Pork

PREP TIME: **30 minutes + 2 hours to marinate** // COOK TIME: **10 minutes** // SERVES: **10**

I really didn't want to start with the typical "When I was a kid..." story but honestly, the best dining out experience from my childhood (and probably most Korean childhoods) involved marinated BBQ pork. Grilled over charcoal, this slightly sweet yet savory BBQ pork was a top Korean barbecue experience for everyone. And I really hope that this delightful experience continues with you.

4½ lb (2kg) Boston butt, cut into ½-inch (1.25cm) slices and scored on both sides
2 tbsp neutral-tasting oil, divided, plus more if needed
1 yellow onion, thinly sliced
1 green onion, thinly sliced, to garnish
1 tsp toasted sesame seeds, to garnish

FOR THE MARINADE

1 large yellow onion, cut into small pieces
6 green onions (100g), cut into small pieces
½ Korean pear (250g) or Asian/Nashi pear or red apple, peeled and cut into small pieces
1 red apple (300g), peeled and cut into small pieces
1½ cups water
1 cup soy sauce
½ cup mirin
2½ tbsp oyster sauce
3 tbsp light corn syrup (or honey)
3 tbsp toasted sesame oil
3 tbsp minced garlic
½ tbsp grated ginger
1 tsp black pepper
1½ tbsp dark soy sauce
½ cup dark brown sugar (or granulated sugar)
1 tsp MSG (optional)

1. To prepare the marinade, to a blender, add the onion, green onions, pear, apple, and water. Blend on high until completely smooth.
2. In a large bowl, stir together the blended mixture with the remaining marinade ingredients.
3. To the marinade, add the pork pieces one by one. Cover the mixing bowl with a lid or plastic wrap and marinate in the fridge for at least 4 hours or overnight (see note).
4. To a large pan, add a tablespoon of oil. Coat the bottom of the pan with a light layer of the oil using a folded paper towel. Heat over medium-high heat. Once it gets nice and hot, add 2 or 3 pork pieces and cook for 5 to 6 minutes or until they are nicely charred and cooked through. (If it's about to burn, you can add a little bit more marinade or pour in some water.) Cut the pork pieces into bite-sized pieces with scissors for serving.
5. To serve, in a large cast-iron pan, add the remaining oil and brush to evenly coat. Add the yellow onion and place over low heat for 2 minutes or until it sizzles. Add the pork galbi pieces over the onion and sprinkle with the green onion and sesame seeds. Remove from the heat and serve with hot rice, ssamjang (Korean dipping sauce), lettuce, or your favorite Korean side dishes. Enjoy!

NOTE: The marinated, uncooked dwaeji galbi can be refrigerated for up to 3 days. If you're not planning to cook it all at once, you can portion it into ziptop bags with 1 to 2 ladles of marinade each and store them in the freezer.

GOCHUJANG SAMGYEOPSAL DEOPBAP

Gochujang Korean BBQ Pork Rice

PREP TIME: **20 minutes** // COOK TIME: **20 minutes** // SERVES: **4**

Jeyuk bokkeum, stir-fried spicy pork, is one of the soul foods for Korean people, especially Korean men. I won't explain that reason, but long story short, it's like tteokbokki for Korean women. Anyway, this stir-fried pork belly with gochujang sauce is a fancier version of it. And this upgraded version of Korean soul food will be served with rice and vegetables. Do you want me to explain more, or should we meet the best rice bowl of all time?

½ tbsp neutral-tasting oil
1.3 lb (600g) pork belly, cut into bite-sized pieces
3 garlic cloves, finely chopped
2 green onions, thinly sliced, white and green parts divided
1 tsp toasted sesame oil
5 oz (150g) lettuce leaves, cut into bite-sized pieces
¼ yellow onion, thinly sliced, soaked in cold water for 5 minutes and drained well
4 cups hot cooked rice, about 7 ½ oz (210g) for each serving
2 soft-boiled eggs (optional), to serve
Toasted sesame seeds, to garnish

FOR THE GOCHUJANG BBQ SAUCE

2 tbsp Korean chili paste (gochujang)
1 tbsp Korean chili pepper flakes (gochugaru)
1 tbsp soy sauce
½ tbsp oyster sauce
1 tbsp granulated sugar
1 tbsp light corn syrup or honey
2 tbsp mirin
Freshly cracked black pepper, to taste
1 tbsp water
1 tsp cornstarch
Pinch of MSG (optional)

FOR THE SALAD DRESSING

1 tbsp soy sauce
1½ tbsp white vinegar
½ tbsp granulated sugar
1 tbsp Korean chili pepper flakes (gochugaru)
1 tbsp toasted sesame oil
1 tbsp fish sauce

1. To make the gochujang BBQ sauce, in a small bowl, stir together all the ingredients until fully incorporated. Set aside.
2. To prepare the salad dressing, in a small bowl, whisk together all the ingredients until thoroughly combined. Set aside.
3. In a large pan, heat the oil over high heat. Once it gets nice and hot, add in the pork belly and cook for 4 minutes or until golden brown and crispy.
4. Add the garlic and the white parts of the green onions. Sauté for 1 minute or until fragrant. Reduce the heat to medium-low. Pour the gochujang BBQ sauce over the pork and stir-fry for 1 to 2 minutes or until the pork is beautifully coated. Turn the heat off, add the sesame oil, and give a final mix. Set aside.
5. To a large bowl, add the lettuce, onion, and salad dressing. Gently toss together until the lettuce is beautifully coated. Set aside.
6. To serve, divide the rice evently between four serving plates or bowls. Add a generous amount of the pork and salad. Top with soft-boiled eggs (if using), the green parts of the green onions, and sesame seeds. Enjoy!

CLAIRE SAYS:

Gochujang will never let you down. It's full of umami, spicy, salty, and a little sweet, everything is really well-balanced. If you love eating "ssam," the traditional Korean lettuce wrap, please place a little bit of everything on your spoon and have it all in one bite. If you do, you will experience the magic that this simple rice bowl can bring your favorite Korean BBQ restaurant to your dining room.

CLAIRE SAYS:

While Aaron says you could use chicken breasts instead of thighs, I highly recommend using skin-on chicken thighs for this recipe. When the fat from the skin meets our doenjang, it will truly elevate this dish to the next level. Trust me, it's the unsung hero of this dish.

DOENJANG DAKGUI DEOPBAP

Doenjang BBQ Chicken Rice

PREP TIME: **20 minutes + 30 minutes to marinate + making Pa Muchim** // COOK TIME: **20 minutes** // SERVES: **4**

In my opinion, Maekjeok (soybean paste marinated BBQ pork) is one of the most underrated BBQ meats in the entire BBQ scene, and I'm very glad to introduce it to you here. It's normally made with pork, but I've modified it to use chicken to make this dish even more accessible. Since it's marinated in doenjang, the ultimate umami bomb, you will experience one of the most flavorful, juicy bites you'll ever have. Once you take a bite, you will instantly understand why this dish has maintained its popularity for over 1,500 years.

1.3 lb (600g) boneless, skin-on chicken thighs (or chicken breasts)
½ tbsp neutral-tasting oil, plus more if needed
4 cups hot cooked rice, about 7½ oz (210g) for each serving
1 portion Pa Muchim (page 35)
Toasted sesame seeds, to garnish

FOR THE MARINADE

3 tbsp Korean soybean paste (doenjang)
½ tbsp soy sauce
1 tbsp oyster sauce
1 tbsp granulated sugar
3 tbsp mirin
1 tbsp minced garlic
1 tbsp honey (or light corn syrup)
1 tbsp toasted sesame oil
Freshly cracked black pepper, to taste

1. To prepare the marinade, in a large bowl, whisk together all the ingredients until thoroughly combined. Add the chicken, and massage until evenly coated. Cover with plastic wrap and marinate in the fridge for at least 30 minutes or overnight.
2. To a large pan, add the oil. Coat the bottom of the pan with a light layer of the oil using a folded paper towel. Heat over medium heat. Once it gets nice and hot, add in the marinated chicken skin-side down. Cook for 3 to 4 minutes or until the bottom turns golden brown.
3. Flip and cook the other side of the chicken until cooked through and nicely charred. (To get the best result, work in batches of about 2 servings at a time. You may need to add more oil to the pan between batches.) Transfer to a cutting board and slice into bite-sized pieces.
4. To serve, divide the rice evenly between four plates or into serving bowls. Add a quarter of the chicken to each plate or bowl and garnish with the Pa Muchim. Sprinkle with sesame seeds. Enjoy!

ONE-PAN JAPCHAE

One-Pan Glass Noodle Stir-Fry

PREP TIME: **30 minutes** // COOK TIME: **10 minutes** // SERVES: **2**

To be honest, I developed this one-pan japchae recipe specifically as an easy weeknight dinner option for myself. You know Claire is the biggest fan of japchae. However, after some experimenting, it turned out that this practical approach could indeed result in an exceptionally delicious japchae. Don't underestimate it just because it's a one-pan recipe. I can confidently say it might just be the most delicious japchae you could ever imagine.

---

4 oz (120g) dangmyeon noodles (Korean sweet potato noodles)
2 tbsp neutral-tasting oil
½ lb (200g) pork loin, cut into 2-inch (5cm) strips
Kosher salt, to taste
Freshly cracked black pepper, to taste
3 garlic cloves, finely chopped
½ yellow onion, thinly sliced
⅓ carrot (60g), cut into thin matchsticks
2 shiitake mushrooms, thinly sliced
¼ yellow bell pepper, julienned
¼ red bell pepper, julienned
2 oz (60g) garlic chives, cut into 2-inch (5cm) pieces
1 tbsp toasted sesame oil
Generous pinch of toasted sesame seeds, to garnish

FOR THE JAPCHAE SAUCE

1½ tbsp soy sauce
1 tbsp oyster sauce
1 tbsp granulated sugar
Pinch of MSG (optional)
⅓ cup water

1. Soak the noodles in warm water for 30 minutes or until soft and bendable. If the noodles are too long, cut them with scissors to about 8 inches (20cm) long.
2. To make the japchae sauce, in a small bowl, add all the ingredients. Mix until thoroughly combined and set aside.
3. In a large pan, heat the oil over medium-high heat. Once it gets nice and hot, add the pork and salt and pepper to taste. Cook for 2 minutes or until no longer pink.
4. Reduce the heat to medium. Add the chopped garlic, onion, carrot, and mushrooms and stir-fry for 3 minutes or until the vegetables are slightly softened. Add the drained noodles and japchae sauce and stir-fry for 3 minutes or until the noodles are fully coated with the sauce.
5. Once most of the liquid has evaporated and the noodles are cooked through, reduce the heat to low, add the bell peppers and garlic chives, and toss together for 1 minute. Turn off the heat. Add the sesame oil and sesame seeds. Give a final mix. Transfer to a serving plate and enjoy!

CLAIRE SAYS:

Japchae is a kind of party food for special occasions like holidays, so large-batch recipes are very common. However, cooking a big batch can often lead to overcooked, mushy japchae. But with this method, you can easily achieve perfectly cooked japchae right at home! Yes, thanks to this recipe, even I (not the best cook) finally have the confidence to serve it to my family and friends. Thanks, Aaron!

CLAIRE SAYS:

Typically, spicy japchae is made using fish cake as a main ingredient. But for someone like me, who is not a big fan of fish cake, Aaron made this version instead. I have a feeling many of you might also prefer this to the fish cake version! And for the best experience, try serving it with some kimchi on the side. That refreshing taste and tanginess from the kimchi really elevates the flavors!

MAEUN JAPCHAE

Spicy Korean Glass Noodle Stir-Fry

PREP TIME: **30 minutes** // COOK TIME: **10 minutes** // SERVES: **2**

Want to know a little secret? This spicy japchae is actually one of my personal favorite variations of the dish. It should have been included in my previous cookbook, *Simply Korean*, but I forgot to add it! So, three years ago, I made a little note to myself not to forget it for my next book. This spicy, savory stir-fried noodle dish is something every Korean food lover should try.

---

4 oz (120g) dangmyeon noodles (Korean sweet potato noodles)
½ tbsp neutral-tasting oil
9 oz (250g) pork belly or pork shoulder, cut into 2-inch (5cm) strips
Kosher salt, to taste
Freshly cracked black pepper, to taste
3 garlic cloves, finely chopped
½ yellow onion, thinly sliced
⅓ carrot (60g), cut into thin matchsticks
2 shiitake mushrooms, thinly sliced
¼ yellow bell pepper, julienned
¼ red bell pepper, julienned
2 oz (60g) garlic chives, cut into 2-inch (5cm) pieces
1 tbsp toasted sesame oil
Generous pinch of toasted sesame seeds, to garnish

FOR THE SPICY JAPCHAE SAUCE

1½ tbsp Korean chili pepper flakes (gochugaru)
1 tbsp Korean chili paste (gochujang)
1 tbsp soy sauce
1 tbsp oyster sauce
1 tbsp mirin
1 tbsp granulated sugar
⅓ cup water

1. Soak the noodles in warm water for 30 minutes or until soft and bendable. If the noodles are too long, cut them with scissors to about 8 inches (20cm) long.
2. To make the spicy japchae sauce, to a small bowl, add all the ingredients. Mix until thoroughly combined and set aside.
3. In a large pan, heat the oil over medium-high heat. Once it gets nice and hot, add the pork and salt and pepper to taste. Cook for 3 or 4 minutes or until golden brown. (If you are using a leaner cut of meat and there is not enough fat in the pan, add 1-2 tablespoons of oil.)
4. Reduce the heat to medium. Add the garlic, onion, carrot, and mushrooms. Stir-fry for 2 minutes or until the vegetables are slightly softened. Add the drained noodles and spicy japchae sauce. Stir-fry for 3 minutes or until the noodles are fully coated with the sauce.
5. When the noodles are cooked through, reduce the heat to low and add the bell peppers and garlic chives. Toss together for 1 minute. Turn off the heat, add the sesame oil, and stir. Taste and add salt if needed. Transfer to a serving plate and finish off with toasted sesame seeds.

DAKKALGUKSU

Korean Chicken Noodle Soup

PREP TIME: **20 minutes** // COOK TIME: **30 minutes** // SERVES: **2**

This chicken noodle soup is the first thing that comes to my mind as soon as the weather gets chilly. With its soft and chewy knife-cut noodles submerged in a rich, flavorful chicken broth, it's the ultimate comfort for a cold winter day. Trust me. When the weather turns cold again, this soup will be calling your name.

½ tbsp neutral-tasting oil
12 oz (350g) boneless, skin-on chicken thighs
½ yellow onion, thinly sliced
7 cups water, divided
½ Yukon Gold potato, cut into thin matchsticks
⅛ carrot (20g), cut into thin matchsticks
2 shiitake mushrooms, thinly sliced
1½ tbsp chicken bouillon powder
1 tbsp fish sauce
2 servings fresh or dried kalguksu noodles (Korean knife-cut noodles)
3 green onions, thinly sliced
3 garlic cloves, finely chopped
Freshly cracked black pepper, to serve

FOR THE SEASONING SAUCE

3 tbsp soy sauce
½ tbsp mirin (optional)
1 tbsp Korean chili pepper flakes (gochugaru)
1 tsp toasted sesame oil
Freshly cracked black pepper, to taste
1 green onion, thinly sliced
1 garlic clove, finely chopped
1 spicy green chili pepper (optional), thinly sliced
1 mild red chili pepper (optional), thinly sliced

1. To make the seasoning sauce, to a small bowl, add all the ingredients. Mix until thoroughly combined and set aside.
2. In a large pot or wok, heat the oil over medium-high heat. Once it gets nice and hot, place the chicken skin-side down in the pan. Cook for 4 minutes or until the chicken is nicely browned on the bottom. Flip the chicken pieces and add the sliced onion and sauté for 4 to 5 minutes. Meanwhile, cut the chicken into bite-sized pieces with tongs and scissors.
3. Once the chicken pieces and the onion are browned, add 4 cups of water and bring to a boil.
4. Once it begins to bubble, add the potato, carrot, mushrooms, chicken bouillon powder, and fish sauce. Simmer for 3 more minutes. Add the remaining 3 cups of water and bring to a boil.
5. When the broth starts bubbling again, untangle the fresh kalguksu noodles, quickly rinse off the starch under cold water, and immediately add to the broth (see note). Cook according to the package instructions. (If you are using dried noodles, cook them in a separate pot and add them to the broth.)
6. Once the noodles are cooked, turn the heat off. Add the green onions and garlic and stir.
7. Divide the noodles evenly between two individual serving bowls. Pour a generous amount of the soup over the noodles and add some black pepper. Serve with the seasoning sauce and kimchi on the side. Enjoy!

NOTE: Fresh kalguksu noodles are covered with lots of starch or flour to prevent them from sticking together. If this starch isn't removed before cooking, the broth may become overly thick.

CLAIRE SAYS:

If you add too much seasoning sauce all at once, the soup might become overly salty. Therefore, it's best to add the sauce gradually, starting with 1 teaspoon, adding more to suit your taste. Also, the sauce may be a little spicy, so I don't recommend adding it to the noodle soup for children.

CLAIRE SAYS:

This noodle soup is a chicken variation of yukgaejang kalguksu, the Korean spicy beef noodle soup you might already know and love. Just like yukgaejang, it pairs perfectly not only with noodles but also with rice, so feel free to enjoy it however you like. You can't go wrong either way!

DAKGAEJANG KALGUKSU

Spicy Chicken Noodle Soup

PREP TIME: **20 minutes** // COOK TIME: **20 minutes** // SERVES: **2**

I'm a huge fan of Korean instant ramyeon. I'm not 100% sure, but I've probably had more than 10,000 bowls in my entire life. And I can say this is the ultimate upgraded version of it. If you can invest just a little more time than it takes to make instant ramyeon, you should definitely give this a try. You won't regret it.

- 1 tbsp neutral-tasting oil
- 1 boneless, skin-on chicken thigh (about 6 oz/170g), cut into bite-sized pieces
- 1 boneless, skinless chicken breast (about 6 oz/170g), cut into bite-sized pieces
- 7 oz (200g) Korean radish (or daikon), peeled and julienned
- 4 green onions, cut into 2-inch (5cm) pieces, plus more to garnish
- 5 cups water
- 4 oz (110g) mung bean sprouts
- 3 shiitake mushrooms, thinly sliced
- 1 green chili pepper (optional), thinly sliced
- Kosher salt, to taste
- 2 servings fresh or dried kalguksu noodles (Korean knife-cut noodles)

FOR THE SEASONING PASTE

- 3 tbsp Korean chili pepper flakes (gochugaru)
- 1 tbsp soy sauce
- 1 tbsp fish sauce
- 1½ tbsp chicken bouillon powder
- 1 tbsp minced garlic
- 1 tbsp toasted sesame oil
- ¼ tsp freshly cracked black pepper

1. To make the seasoning paste, in a small bowl, combine all the ingredients. Mix until thoroughly combined and set aside.
2. In a large pot or wok, heat the oil over medium-high heat. Once it gets nice and hot, place the chicken inside and cook for 3 to 4 minutes or until the chicken is nicely browned. When the fat is rendered, add the radish and green onions. Sauté for 2 minutes or until the vegetables are starting to soften.
3. Reduce the heat to medium-low, add the seasoning paste, and gently stir-fry for 2 minutes or until everything is fully coated with the seasoning paste and chili oil.
4. Add the water and bring to a boil. Add the mung bean sprouts, mushrooms, and chili pepper (if using). Let simmer for 7 minutes over medium-high heat, uncovered. Taste and add salt if needed.
5. While the broth is simmering, untangle the fresh kalguksu noodles and quickly rinse under cold water to remove the starch (see note). Immediately cook the noodles in a separate pot of boiling water according to the package instructions.
6. Divide the cooked noodles evenly among two individual serving bowls and pour a generous amount of broth over the noodles. Garnish with sliced green onions. Enjoy with kimchi on the side.

NOTE: Fresh kalguksu noodles are covered with lots of starch or flour to prevent them from sticking together. If this starch isn't removed before cooking, the broth may become overly thick.

JANG KALGUKSU

Gochujang Noodle Soup

PREP TIME: **20 minutes** // COOK TIME: **20 minutes** // SERVES: **2**

If you opened this book hoping for the best gochujang stew recipe, you might be a little disappointed. I'm sorry! The ultimate gochujang stew recipe is already in my previous cookbook, *Simply Korean*, so there's nothing much I can do about it. But don't worry about that. This Jang Kalguksu, with its rich, hearty, savory gochujang-based broth and satisfying noodles, will take care of everything. You might even forget all about gochujang stew and start craving only this one!

---

2 tbsp neutral-tasting oil
5 oz (150g) ground beef
½ tbsp soy sauce
1 tsp granulated sugar
Freshly cracked black pepper, to taste
4 green onions, thinly sliced, white and green parts divided
2 garlic cloves, finely chopped
3 tbsp Korean chili paste (gochujang)
1 tbsp Korean soybean paste (doenjang)
1 tbsp Korean chili pepper flakes (gochugaru)
6 cups water
½ Yukon Gold potato, julienned
2 shiitake mushrooms, thinly sliced
½ yellow onion, thinly sliced
1 tbsp Korean beef stock powder (Dasida) or chicken bouillon powder
¼ tsp MSG (optional)
2 servings fresh or dried kalguksu noodles (Korean knife-cut noodles)
¼ zucchini, julienned
1 green chili pepper (optional), thinly sliced
Toasted seasoned seaweed (optional), cut into thin strips, to garnish
2 tbsp toasted ground sesame seeds, to garnish

1. In a large pot, heat the oil over medium heat. Once it gets nice and hot, add the ground beef. Break up the beef and sauté for 1 to 2 minutes or until no longer pink.
2. Add the soy sauce, sugar, and black pepper. Stir everything together for 1 minute. Reduce the heat to low. Add the white parts of the green onions, garlic, Korean chili paste, Korean soybean paste, and Korean chili pepper flakes. Stir-fry for 3 minutes or until you can see the beautiful chili oil on the surface. (Chili paste and flakes burn easily, so make sure to keep stirring to prevent them from burning.)
3. Add the water and bring to a boil over medium-high heat. Once bubbling away, add the potato, mushrooms, yellow onion, Korean beef stock powder, and MSG (if using). Simmer for 3 to 4 minutes or until the potatoes are halfway cooked.
4. While the broth is simmering, untangle the fresh kalguksu noodles, quickly rinse them under cold water to remove the starch, and immediately add to the broth (see note). Cook according to the package instructions. Add the zucchini and chili pepper (if using) and cook for 1 more minute. (If you are using dried noodles, cook them in a separate pot and add them to the broth.)
5. Divide the noodles evenly among two individual serving bowls and pour a generous amount of the soup over the noodles. Garnish with the toasted seasoned seaweed (if using), the green parts of the green onions, and sesame seeds. Serve immediately.

NOTE: Fresh kalguksu noodles are covered with lots of starch or flour to prevent them from sticking together. If this starch isn't removed before cooking, the broth may become overly thick.

CLAIRE SAYS:

You might think this noodle soup is extremely spicy just because it has gochujang in it, but it's actually nice and comforting. If you're experiencing the worst hangover, give this a try. Trust me. It might make you forget about the pain from the hangover and make you drink again. FYI, this is what I've heard— I don't drink!

CLAIRE SAYS:

I'm really disappointed there's no tteokguk (Korean rice cake soup) recipe in this book. But I have a solution. You can simply replace the kalguksu noodles with thinly sliced rice cakes. That deep, rich, and beefy broth will work perfectly with rice cakes, and you will likely end up with the most amazing tteokguk you've ever had.

KALMANDUGUK

Dumpling Noodle Soup

PREP TIME: **20 minutes** // COOK TIME: **20 minutes** // SERVES: **2**

Let me guess. If you've ever traveled to South Korea, you've probably visited the popular tourist spot, Myeong-dong. And I bet you stepped into a very famous restaurant there to try this dish. Do you miss that incredible noodle soup that warmed your body and soul? Are you eager to visit again? From now on, you don't have to worry about that. With this recipe, you can bring that unforgettable experience right into your kitchen. And I think I saved you thousands of dollars. You're welcome!

---

1 tbsp neutral-tasting oil
3 green onions, thinly sliced, white and green parts divided
7 oz (200g) ground beef
1 tsp granulated sugar
2 tbsp soy sauce, divided
6 cups water
2 garlic cloves, finely chopped
1 tbsp fish sauce
1 tbsp Korean beef stock powder (Dasida) or chicken bouillon powder
Pinch of MSG (optional)
8 dumplings (or frozen dumplings)
Kosher salt, to taste
2 servings fresh or dried kalguksu noodles (Korean knife-cut noodles)
½ oz (15g) garlic chives (optional), cut into 2-inch (5cm) pieces
½ mild green chili pepper (optional), thinly sliced, to garnish
½ mild red chili pepper (optional), thinly sliced, to garnish
Freshly cracked black pepper, to taste

1. In a large pot, heat the oil over medium heat. Once it gets nice and hot, add the white parts of the green onions and sauté for 1 minute or until fragrant.
2. Increase the heat to high. Add the ground beef. Break up the beef and cook for 1 to 2 minutes or until no longer pink. Add the sugar and 1 tablespoon of the soy sauce and sauté for 1 minute or until most of the fat has rendered out. Turn the heat off. Take half of the beef from the pot and set aside for topping.
3. To the same pot, add the water, garlic, remaining tablespoon of soy sauce, fish sauce, Korean beef stock powder, and MSG (if using). Bring to a boil.
4. Once the broth starts to boil, throw in the dumplings. Cover and cook for 5 minutes or until the dumplings are cooked through. Taste and add more salt if needed.
5. While the broth is simmering, untangle the fresh kalguksu noodles and quickly rinse under cold water to remove the starch (see note). Immediately cook the noodles in a separate medium pot of boiling water according to the package instructions.
6. Divide the noodles evenly among two individual serving bowls and pour a generous amount of the soup over the noodles. Top with the dumplings, garlic chives (if using), beef topping, green parts of the green onions, and chili peppers (if using), and finish with black pepper. Serve immediately. Enjoy with kimchi on the side.

NOTE: Fresh kalguksu noodles are covered with lots of starch or flour to prevent them from sticking together. If this starch isn't removed before cooking, the broth may become overly thick.

YURINGI

Korean-Chinese Style Fried Chicken Salad

PREP TIME: **20 minutes + 10 minutes to marinate** // COOK TIME: **20 minutes** // SERVES: **3–4**

We always hear: Eat lots of vegetables for your health. But it's not easy, right? With this Korean-Chinese style fried chicken salad, you might find yourself eating as much as an elephant. Trust me. The combination of crispy fried chicken and crunchy vegetables, all doused in a sweet and sour dressing, will absolutely blow your mind.

---

17 oz (500g) boneless, skin-on chicken thighs (or chicken breasts)
High-heat oil (such as canola, avocado, vegetable oil, etc.), for frying
¼ head iceberg lettuce, shredded
1 large green onion (or 2–3 regular green onions), shredded, soaked in cold water and drained well

FOR THE MARINADE

½ tbsp soy sauce
½ tbsp mirin (or sake, dry sherry, soju, Shaoxing wine, etc.)
¼ tsp white pepper (or black pepper)

FOR THE DRESSING

5 tbsp water
3½ tbsp soy sauce
3 tbsp granulated sugar
4 tbsp white vinegar
1 tsp chicken bouillon powder
1 tsp toasted sesame oil
1 garlic clove, finely chopped
2 mild red chili peppers, thinly sliced
3 green chili peppers, thinly sliced
(Cheongyang chili peppers [Korean spicy chili peppers] are usually used for that spicy kick, but you can use a mix of red and green bell peppers to reduce the heat instead.)

FOR THE BATTER

1 cup potato starch (or sweet potato starch, cornstarch)
½ cup water
2 tbsp neutral oil
1 egg white

1. Using a knife, try to flatten the chicken as evenly as possible. Make a few small cuts along the edges to prevent the chicken from curling while it's frying. Transfer to a bowl. (You can also smack the chicken thighs a few times with the back of the knife. If you are using chicken breasts, use a meat mallet to pound them flat.)
2. Add all the marinade ingredients to the chicken and gently massage until evenly coated. Cover and marinate in the fridge for 10 minutes.
3. To make the dressing, in a small bowl, combine all the ingredients. Mix until the sugar is dissolved and set aside.
4. To prepare the batter, in a medium bowl, add all the batter ingredients. Whisk together until smooth and lump-free. Set aside.
5. Fill a wok or heavy-bottomed pot with the oil. (Do not fill the pot more than ¾ full.) Heat over medium-high until it reaches 340°F (170°C).
6. Once the oil has reached the right temperature, give the batter a quick stir, dip the chicken into the batter, and carefully drop it into the oil. Fry, turning occasionally, for 3 to 4 minutes until light brown. Repeat with the remaining chicken pieces. (The chicken pieces might stick together, but don't try to separate them in the oil. Otherwise, you might see some naked chicken pieces at the end.)
7. Remove the chicken from the oil with a strainer. Smash the chicken pieces with a spatula. This will not only separate them from each other, it will also help remove some of the moisture that's trapped inside and make them more crispy.
8. Increase the oil temperature to 355°F (180°C). Fry the chicken pieces a second time for 3 more minutes or until golden brown and cooked through. Transfer to a cooling rack and repeat with the remaining chicken pieces. Slice the fried chicken into bite-sized strips.
9. To serve, place the shredded lettuce onto a serving plate. Top with the sliced fried chicken and add a generous amount of dressing over the top. Garnish with the green onion. Serve with hot rice, noodle dishes, or your favorite drinks. Enjoy!

CLAIRE SAYS:

Most of you already know that Koreans love pairing crispy fried chicken with an ice-cold beer. That's because it's the perfect way to unwind after a long day at work. And obviously, this Yuringi with a cold beer is one of the best pairings of all time. Once you try this combination, you will understand what I'm talking about.

JAENGBAN JJAJANG

Stir-Fried Noodles with Black Bean Sauce

PREP TIME: **15 minutes** // COOK TIME: **20 minutes** // SERVES: **2**

If you are looking for the classic jjajangmyeon recipe (noodles with black bean sauce), I'm so sorry. I won't put that recipe here because it is already in *Simply Korean*. But don't worry about it! Let me show you one of the best variations of jjajangmyeon. It's distinctively served on a large plate with a variety of seafood or other toppings. Yes, it is the fancier version that you've always dreamed of.

CLAIRE SAYS:

There might be some people who have never tried jjajangmyeon, but I don't think there is a person who has tried it only once. Yes, it's that addictive! However, because of that reason, if you have eaten it millions of times, you might want something different, so please sprinkle some Korean chili pepper flakes (gochugaru) on top and try. That will add a nice little kick to it.

2 tbsp neutral-tasting oil
1 tbsp lard (optional)
4 oz (120g) pork belly (or beef or chicken), cut into bite-sized pieces
1 tsp freshly grated ginger
1 tbsp soy sauce
1 large yellow onion, diced
3 green onions, thinly sliced
1 cup fresh or frozen raw seafood mix (80g shrimp, 80g squid), blanched
6 white button mushrooms, cut into quarters
1½ tbsp granulated sugar
1 tbsp oyster sauce
1 tbsp chicken bouillon powder
½ tsp MSG (optional)
½ cup + 1 tbsp water, divided
1 tsp cornstarch
2 servings jjajangmyeon noodles (or kalguksu, udon noodles, etc.)
1 oz (30g) garlic chives, cut into 2-inch (5cm) pieces
1 tbsp toasted sesame oil
⅓ English cucumber (optional), julienned, to serve
2 fried eggs (optional), to serve

FOR THE BLACK BEAN PASTE

½ cup neutral-tasting oil
1 cup (250g) black bean paste (chunjang; be sure to use a Korean paste)

1. To prepare the black bean paste, in a medium nonstick wok or skillet, combine the oil and black bean paste. Cook over medium heat, stirring constantly, for 2 minutes or until bubbling. Transfer to a food storage container and let cool completely before covering with a lid. Set aside.
2. In a large wok or pan over medium heat, heat the oil and lard (if using). Add the pork belly and render out the fat for 2 to 3 minutes. Once the pork is nicely browned, add the ginger and stir-fry for 30 seconds. Add the soy sauce and stir for 1 minute. (Be careful of oil splatter when you add the soy sauce.)
3. Increase the heat to high. Add the yellow onion and green onions. Stir-fry for 2 minutes or until the vegetables are slightly softened.
4. Add the blanched seafood, mushrooms, sugar, oyster sauce, chicken bouillon powder, and MSG (if using). Stir-fry for another 2 minutes.
5. Add 1½ tablespoons of the fried black bean paste and stir it all together for 2 minutes or until everything is well coated. Reduce the heat to medium, add ½ cup of water, and bring it to a boil.
6. Meanwhile, in a small bowl, mix the cornstarch with the remaining tablespoon of water.
7. Once the sauce comes to a boil, add the cornstarch slurry and immediately stir until the sauce is slightly thickened and shiny. Cover and keep warm until the noodles are ready.
8. In a large pot of boiling water, cook the noodles according to the package instructions. Rinse the cooked noodles thoroughly under cold water and drain well.
9. Bring the sauce to a boil over high heat and add the drained noodles. Toss together for 1 to 2 minutes or until thoroughly combined. Turn the heat off. Add the garlic chives and drizzle with the sesame oil. Give a final mix.
10. Transfer to a large platter. Top with the julienned cucumber and some fried eggs, if using. Enjoy with yellow pickled radish (danmuji) or kimchi on the side.

NOTE: The fried black bean paste can be refrigerated for up to 2 weeks.

SACHEON JJAJANG

Spicy Jjajangmyeon

PREP TIME: **20 minutes** // COOK TIME: **25 minutes** // SERVES: **3**

In Korean-Chinese cuisine, when a dish is spicy and red, it's often referred to as "Sacheon (Sichuan-style) blah blah," and the same goes for this spicy style of jjajangmyeon. Despite its name, this dish has no real connection to the Sichuan region. But what does that matter? Food always evolves through various experiments into different styles and this dish is no exception. By the way, if you're a fan of mapo tofu and jjajangmyeon, you will absolutely love this dish.

---

2 tbsp chili oil (or neutral-tasting oil)
10½ oz (300g) pork belly or pork shoulder, cut into small, bite-sized pieces
4 green onions, thinly sliced
2 garlic cloves, finely chopped
1 tsp freshly grated ginger
1 large yellow onion, cut into bite-sized pieces
2–3 green cabbage leaves (100g), cut into bite-sized pieces
1½ tbsp cornstarch
4 tbsp water
1 tsp Sichuan peppercorn oil (optional)
3 servings jjajangmyeon noodles (or kalguksu, udon noodles, etc.)
⅓ English cucumber (optional), julienned, to serve
3 fried eggs (optional), to serve

FOR THE SAUCE

1 tbsp Korean chili pepper flakes (gochugaru)
1½ tbsp Chinese chili bean paste (doubanjiang)
2 tbsp soy sauce
1 tbsp oyster sauce
1 tbsp chicken bouillon powder
1 tbsp granulated sugar
1 tbsp mirin

1. To make the sauce, in a small bowl, stir together all the ingredients until fully incorporated. (You can reduce the Korean chili pepper flakes or Chinese chili bean paste to make it less spicy.) Set aside.
2. In a large wok or pan, heat the chili oil over high heat. Add the pork and cook for 1 to 2 minutes. Once the pork is no longer pink, add the green onions, garlic, and ginger. Sauté for 1 to 2 minutes or until fragrant. Add the onion and cabbage and stir-fry for 2 minutes or until the vegetables are slightly softened. Pour in the sauce and stir-fry for 2 minutes or until thoroughly combined.
3. In a small bowl, mix the cornstarch with the water. Add the slurry to the wok and immediately stir until the sauce is thickened and shiny, about 1 minute. Add the Sichuan peppercorn oil (if using) and give a final mix. Keep warm until ready to serve.
4. In a large pot of boiling water, cook the noodles according to the package instructions. Drain and rinse the cooked noodles well under cold water.
5. Divide the noodles evenly among three individual serving bowls and top with the sauce. Serve with the julienned cucumber (if using) and a fried egg (if using). Enjoy with yellow pickled radish (danmuji) or kimchi on the side.

CLAIRE SAYS:

When trying jjajangmyeon for the first time, some people don't mix it thoroughly—but doing it that way, you miss out on the full flavor. Before taking a bite, be sure every single noodle is well-coated in the sauce. Trust me, it'll make a huge difference in taste!

CLAIRE SAYS:

Aaron and I have always felt that jjamppong is one of the best noodle soups in Korea. It's a bit surprising that it isn't more popular internationally—maybe because of the less-than-tempting translation of "spicy seafood noodle soup." But this brisket-based jjamppong is a whole different story, with simple ingredients and an easy cooking process. Once you try it, you might not find yourself reaching for Korean instant noodles anymore.

CHADOL JJAMPPONG

Spicy Noodle Soup with Beef Brisket

PREP TIME: **20 minutes** // COOK TIME: **20 minutes** // SERVES: **2**

If I had to pick just one noodle soup to recommend for you guys to try in Korea, I would definitely pick jjamppong. However, jjamppong is made with seafood, so some of you might not like it—even though it doesn't taste fishy at all. However, since this version is made with beef brisket, I think nobody can say no to this. Super cool, right?

---

2 tbsp neutral-tasting oil
9 oz (250g) frozen pre-sliced beef brisket (chadolbagi) or any steak, thinly sliced
2 green onions, the tops cut into 2-inch (5cm) pieces, plus thinly sliced white parts
4 garlic cloves, finely chopped
1 Vietnamese dried chili (or peperoncino) (optional)
1 tbsp soy sauce
1 yellow onion, cut into ½-inch (1.25cm) slices
2 Napa cabbage leaves or green cabbage leaves, cut into bite-sized pieces
1 baby bok choy, cut into quarters lengthwise
2½ tbsp fine Korean chili pepper flakes (gochugaru)
1 tbsp oyster sauce
1 tbsp chicken bouillon powder
4½ cups water, divided
½ tsp white pepper (or black pepper)
2 servings of jjajangmyeon noodles (or udon noodles)
Kosher salt, to taste
Shredded green onions (optional), to garnish

1. In a large wok or pot, heat the oil over medium-high heat. Add the brisket and cook for 2 minutes or until the fat is rendered out. Add the white parts of the green onions, garlic, and dried chili (if using). Sauté for 1 minute or until fragrant. Add the soy sauce and stir for 30 seconds. (Be careful of oil splatter when you add the soy sauce.)
2. Add the onion, cabbage, and baby bok choy. Give a few stirs. Add the Korean chili pepper flakes, oyster sauce, and chicken bouillon powder. Stir-fry for 2 minutes or until you get a beautiful red color.
3. Increase the heat to high. Add 2 cups of water and bring to a boil. Let simmer for 1 minute. Add the remaining 2½ cups of water and bring to a boil again. Once it is bubbling, add the green parts of the green onions and white pepper and simmer for 3 more minutes.
4. While the soup is simmering, cook the noodles in a separate pot of water according to the package instructions. Rinse the cooked noodles well under cold water to get rid of excess starch.
5. Give the soup a quick taste and add salt to taste. Divide the noodles evenly between two individual serving bowls. Pour a generous amount of the soup over the noodles, top with shredded green onions (if using), and serve immediately.

NOTE: When cooking jjamppong, it is best to use fine gochugaru because it dissolves more easily into the broth, ensuring that the flavor and color are evenly distributed throughout the dish. If you only have coarse gochugaru, try grinding it in a blender. Although it won't be as fine as powder, you will get a pretty good result.

KOREAN FUSION

BOKKEUM UDON

5-Minute Spicy Udon Stir-Fry

PREP TIME: **3 minutes** // COOK TIME: **5 minutes** // SERVES: **1**

As you all know, I've shared a variety of quick and easy recipes on my YouTube channel, many of which are titled "...that even college students can make." Among those, I think this recipe takes the crown—I'd like to call it: "5-Minute Spicy Udon Stir-Fry That Even Elementary School Students Can Make."

---

1 serving udon noodles (or spaghetti, fettuccine, etc.)
1 tbsp neutral-tasting oil
4 oz (120g) ground pork
1 green onion, thinly sliced, white and green parts divided
Kosher salt and black pepper, to taste
Generous pinch of toasted sesame seeds

FOR THE SAUCE

1 tbsp Korean chili pepper flakes (gochugaru)
1 tbsp soy sauce
1 tbsp oyster sauce
1 tbsp granulated sugar
5 tbsp water

1. To make the sauce, in a small bowl, combine all the ingredients. Mix until thoroughly combined and set aside.
2. Bring a pot of water to a boil. Once boiling, cook the noodles according to the package instructions. Once the noodles are cooked, drain and set them aside.
3. Meanwhile, in a wok or medium pan, heat the oil over medium heat. Once it gets nice and hot, add the pork, white parts of the green onions, salt, and pepper. Break up the pork and sauté for 3 minutes or until the pork is fully cooked.
4. Add the sauce and stir to combine. Add in the noodles and stir-fry for 1 to 2 minutes or until they are fully coated. (You can add some reserved cooking water from the noodles, if needed, to achieve your desired consistency.)
5. Once most of the liquid has evaporated, turn off the heat. Transfer to a serving bowl and finish with sesame seeds and the green parts of the green onion. Serve immediately and enjoy!

CLAIRE SAYS:

This spicy, savory, and slightly sweet stir-fried noodle dish is one of my favorite quick and easy meals. On those days when you don't even want to lift a finger, this is the fastest, most delicious, and most satisfying meal you can make. Plus, the cleanup is a breeze—just a pan, a serving bowl, and a pair of chopsticks. Trust me, for a busy weeknight, there's no better option than this.

CLAIRE SAYS:

This ground beef bulgogi is really good for weekly meal prep. You can store it in an airtight container in the fridge. It will last up to 3 days there or for a few months in the freezer. Make sure to cool completely before you store them.

DAJIN SOGOGI BULGOGI

Ground Beef Bulgogi

PREP TIME: **20 minutes + 15 minutes to marinate** // COOK TIME: **15 minutes** // SERVES: **5**

Traditionally, Koreans don't make bulgogi with ground beef. However, if we can enjoy bulgogi that is faster, easier, and even tastier on a busy weeknight, I'm willing to compromise a little on tradition. I'm sure you would, too. Trust me. This ground beef bulgogi will be the game-changer for your busy weeknight dinners.

1.3 lb (600g) ground beef
2 shiitake mushrooms (or button mushrooms), about 2 oz (50g) in total, finely chopped
2 tbsp neutral-tasting oil
2 green onions, thinly sliced, white and green parts divided, plus more to garnish
½ yellow onion, finely diced
1 green chili pepper (optional), thinly sliced
1 mild red chili pepper (optional), thinly sliced
½ tbsp toasted sesame oil
5 cups hot cooked rice, about 7½ oz (210g) for each serving
Toasted sesame seeds, to garnish

FOR THE BULGOGI MARINADE

3 tbsp soy sauce
2 tbsp granulated sugar
2 tbsp mirin
2 ½ tbsp oyster sauce
2 tbsp minced garlic
1 tbsp toasted sesame oil
Freshly cracked black pepper, to taste
Small pinch of MSG (optional)

1. To make the bulgogi marinade, in a small bowl, combine all the ingredients. Mix until thoroughly combined.
2. To a large bowl, add the ground beef, mushrooms, and marinade, and stir well until thoroughly mixed. Cover with plastic wrap and marinate in the fridge for 15 minutes.
3. In a large wok or pan, heat the oil over medium-high heat. Once it gets nice and hot, add the white parts of the green onions and the yellow onion. Sauté for 3 minutes or until they start to brown.
4. Add the beef mixture and cook for 7 to 8 minutes. Make sure to break up the beef and keep stirring constantly.
5. When the beef is cooked through and most of the liquid has evaporated, turn the heat off. Add the chili peppers (if using), green parts of the green onions, and sesame oil. Give a final mix.
6. To serve, divide the rice evenly between five serving bowls and top with the ground beef bulgogi. Garnish with extra green onions and sesame seeds. Serve with kimchi (pages 36-40), Oi Muchim (page 28), or any salad greens. Enjoy!

DAJIN DWAEJIGOGI BULGOGI

Spicy Ground Pork Bulgogi

PREP TIME: **20 minutes** // COOK TIME: **15 minutes** // SERVES: **5**

Korean bulgogi typically comes in two main types: beef bulgogi, which features a savory soy sauce base, and pork bulgogi, known for its spicy kick from gochugaru or gochujang. If you've already tried the ground beef bulgogi but haven't experienced the spicy pork version, you're missing out on the best dish of your life. Trust me. This spicy yet slightly sweet pork bulgogi is the perfect reward at the end of a long day.

---

1 tbsp neutral-tasting oil
2 green onions, thinly sliced, white and green parts divided, plus more to garnish
½ yellow onion, finely diced
1.3 lb (600g) ground pork
1 green chili pepper (optional), thinly sliced
1 mild red chili pepper (optional), thinly sliced
½ tbsp toasted sesame oil
5 cups hot cooked rice, about 7½ (210g) for each serving
Toasted sesame seeds, to garnish

FOR THE SPICY BULGOGI SAUCE

4 tbsp Korean chili pepper flakes (gochugaru)
3 tbsp soy sauce
2 tbsp granulated sugar
2 tbsp mirin
2½ tbsp oyster sauce
2 tbsp minced garlic
1 tsp minced ginger
Freshly cracked black pepper, to taste
Small pinch of MSG (optional)

1. To make the spicy bulgogi sauce, in a small bowl, combine all the ingredients. Mix until thoroughly combined and set aside.
2. In a large wok or pan, heat the oil over medium-high heat. Once it gets nice and hot, add the white parts of the green onions and the yellow onion. Sauté for 3 minutes or until they start to go brown.
3. Increase the heat to high. Add the pork, break it down, and cook for 3 to 4 minutes or until the pork begins to brown.
4. Once the pork is cooked, add the sauce. Stir-fry for 3 minutes or until everything is beautifully coated with the sauce.
5. When most of the liquid has evaporated, turn the heat off. Add the chili peppers (if using), green parts of the green onions, and sesame oil. Give a final mix.
6. To serve, divide the rice evenly between five serving bowls and top with the ground pork bulgogi. Garnish with extra green onions and sesame seeds. Serve with kimchi (pages 36–40), Oi Muchim (page 28), or any salad greens. Enjoy!

CLAIRE SAYS:

As you guys all know, I'm a huge fan of fried eggs. If you're like me, serve this dish with some fried eggs on the side. They will balance out the flavor and spiciness perfectly.

CLAIRE SAYS:

Just like with other egg rice bowls, I suggest cooking the egg sunny-side up because the runny egg yolk becomes a part of the sauce. If you're not a fan of sunny-side up, don't worry about it. The residual heat from the hot rice and cabbage stir-fry will cook it perfectly.

YANGBAECHU DEOPBAP

Cabbage Rice Bowl with Bacon

PREP TIME: **7 minutes** // COOK TIME: **5 minutes** // SERVES: **1**

This is an incredibly simple yet insanely tasty rice bowl dish. When you're not in the mood to cook but still want a tasty meal, this will likely be the first thing that comes to mind. With ingredients you probably already have at home, it brings together an amazing symphony of flavors.

---

1 tbsp neutral-tasting oil
1 strip uncooked bacon, thinly sliced
1 garlic clove, finely chopped
2 green onions, thinly sliced, plus more to garnish
2 cups green cabbage, thinly sliced
1 tsp soy sauce
½ tbsp oyster sauce
Freshly cracked black pepper, to taste
1 large egg
1 cup hot cooked rice, about 7½ oz (210g)
Generous pinch of toasted sesame seeds, to garnish

1. In a small nonstick pan, heat the oil over medium heat. Add the bacon and cook for 1 minute or until it starts to go brown. Add the garlic and green onions. Sauté for 1 minute or until fragrant.
2. Add the cabbage, soy sauce, oyster sauce, and black pepper. Stir-fry for 2 minutes or until the cabbage is cooked through but still nice and crunchy.
3. Using a spatula, make a little space in the middle. Crack an egg in the empty space and cook to your liking. (Add more oil if needed.)
4. To serve, put the rice into a bowl. Top with the cabbage stir-fry. Garnish with green onions and sesame seeds. Enjoy!

MANEUL BOKKEUMMYEON

Chili Garlic Noodles

PREP TIME: **7 minutes** // COOK TIME: **8 minutes** // SERVES: **2**

After a long day of work, whether you are a beginner or a professional chef, the last thing you want to do is make your own dinner. But with these chili garlic noodles, you will have the simplest, yet most satisfying dinner in just 15 minutes.

---

2 servings Chinese dried knife-sliced noodles (or spaghetti, fettuccine, etc.)
3 tbsp neutral-tasting oil
2 green onions, thinly sliced, white and green parts divided
5–10 garlic cloves, finely chopped
½ tsp freshly grated ginger
7 oz (200g) ground pork
Freshly cracked black pepper, to taste
2 baby bok choy, cut in half or quartered lengthwise and blanched
Toasted sesame seeds, to garnish

FOR THE SAUCE

2–3 tbsp Korean chili pepper flakes (gochugaru)
1 tbsp granulated sugar
2 tbsp soy sauce
2 tbsp oyster sauce
1 tbsp Chinese Shaoxing wine, mirin, or any cooking wine

1. To make the sauce, in a small bowl, combine all the ingredients. Mix until thoroughly combined and set aside.
2. Bring a pot of water to a boil. Once boiling, cook the noodles according to the package instructions.
3. Meanwhile, in a large wok or pan, heat the oil over medium-high heat. Add the white parts of the green onions, garlic, and ginger. Cook for 1 to 2 minutes or until browned and fragrant.
4. Add the ground pork and black pepper. Break up the pork and sauté for 1 to 2 minutes or until no longer pink. Reduce the heat to medium, add in the sauce, and stir-fry for 1 to 2 minutes or until everything is fully coated with the sauce.
5. Add the drained noodles. Stir-fry for 1 to 2 minutes or until the noodles are fully coated. (You can add 1 or 2 tablespoons of reserved noodle cooking water, if needed, to achieve your desired consistency.)
6. Divide the noodles evenly between two serving plates. Top with the baby bok choy, green parts of the green onions, and sesame seeds.

CLAIRE SAYS:

These chili garlic noodles are amazing on their own, but if you add a touch of Chinese spicy chili crisp or black vinegar halfway through, it will feel like you're enjoying three different dishes on the same plate.

CLAIRE SAYS:

For garnish, shishito peppers are Aaron's pick, but feel free to use other green vegetables as well, such as broccoli, green beans, asparagus, Brussels sprouts.

GANJANG DAKGUI

Soy Glazed Chicken

PREP TIME: **15 minutes** // COOK TIME: **20 minutes** // SERVES: **3–4**

I hope every member of your family masters this recipe. There are three reasons for this. First, it's incredibly easy to prepare. Second, it appeals to everyone, no matter their age or preference. Third, it offers an exceptional dining experience, particularly when paired with rice. Indeed! Yes! This fantastic recipe can turn even Claire into a top chef.

1.3 lb (600g) boneless, skin-on chicken thighs
Kosher salt and black pepper, to taste
¼ cup cornstarch, to coat
3 tbsp neutral-tasting oil, divided
5 garlic cloves, finely chopped
2 tsp freshly grated ginger
1 green onion, thinly sliced, white and green parts divided
2 cups shishito peppers, cut into bite-sized pieces
3–4 cups hot cooked rice, about 7½ oz (210g) for each serving
Toasted sesame seeds, to garnish
3–4 soft-boiled eggs (optional), to serve

FOR THE SOY GLAZED SAUCE

2½ tbsp soy sauce
1 tbsp honey
1 tbsp granulated sugar
2 tbsp oyster sauce
1 tbsp mirin or any cooking wine
1 tbsp chicken bouillon powder
1 tsp cornstarch
½ cup water
1 dried chili or peperoncino (optional), finely chopped

1. To make the soy glazed sauce, in a small bowl, combine all the ingredients. Mix until thoroughly combined and set aside.
2. Pat the chicken dry with paper towels. Lightly season both sides with salt and pepper. Coat them with cornstarch, making sure they are evenly coated. Shake off any excess coating.
3. In a large pan, heat 2 tablespoons of oil over medium-high heat. Once it gets nice and hot, place the chicken skin-side down and cook for 4 minutes or until the bottom turns golden brown. Flip and cook the other side for 4 minutes or until the chicken is cooked through. Remove from the pan and set aside.
4. To the same pan, add the garlic, ginger, and white parts of the green onions. Sauté for 30 seconds or until fragrant. Pour in the sauce and bring to a boil over medium-high heat. After 3 minutes, add the chicken back in. Continue flipping the chicken for 2 minutes or until it is thoroughly coated. Set aside.
5. In another medium pan, heat 1 tablespoon of oil over medium-high heat. Once it's heated, add the shishito peppers and salt and pepper to taste. Cook for 3 minutes or until nice and charred.
6. To serve, divide the rice evenly between three or four serving bowls and top with the chicken. Drizzle with some sauce from the pan. Garnish with shishito peppers, sesame seeds, the green parts of the green onion, and soft-boiled eggs (if using).

CHAMCHIJEON

Korean-Style Tuna Pancakes

PREP TIME: **3 minutes** // COOK TIME: **10 minutes** // MAKES: **10**

This might not be the most traditional Korean pancake, but it's still the perfect introduction to the beauty of savory pancakes. It's incredibly easy and simple to make, and it doesn't even require any special or hard-to-find ingredients. Once you try this, you might find yourself craving other Korean pancakes and end up getting *Simply Korean*, which includes lots of Korean pancakes. Thank you in advance!

---

5 oz (135g) canned tuna, drained
1 green onion, finely chopped
¼ yellow onion, finely chopped
⅛ carrot (20g), finely chopped
2 large eggs
2 tbsp all-purpose flour
Kosher salt and black pepper, to taste
2 tbsp neutral-tasting oil, divided
½ green chili pepper (optional), thinly sliced, to garnish
½ mild red chili pepper (optional), thinly sliced, to garnish

FOR THE DIPPING SAUCE

1 tbsp soy sauce
1 tbsp white vinegar
1 tsp Korean chili pepper flakes (gochugaru)
Small pinch of toasted sesame seeds

1. To make the dipping sauce, in a small bowl, combine all the ingredients. Mix until thoroughly combined and set aside.
2. To a medium bowl, add the tuna, green onion, yellow onion, carrot, eggs, flour, salt, and black pepper. Mix together until the batter is thoroughly combined.
3. In a large nonstick pan, heat 1 tablespoon of oil over medium heat. Once it gets nice and hot, add half the batter to the pan in 2-tablespoon portions, or as desired, spacing them far enough apart to avoid them sticking together. Cook for 2 minutes or until the bottom turns golden brown.
4. Place the chili peppers (if using) on the center of the pancakes. Flip and cook the other side for an additional 2 minutes or until golden brown. Transfer to a serving plate and repeat with the remaining pancake batter. Serve warm with the dipping sauce. Enjoy!

CLAIRE SAYS:

If you are not a big fan of canned tuna, don't worry about it. You can simply replace it with ground beef. We call that wanjajeon. While it may not be the perfect wanjajeon recipe, it will still taste delicious!

CLAIRE SAYS:

I do love a classic grilled cheese with American cheese, but I can't forget the moment Aaron made this with Monterey Jack and Gouda. So, try experimenting with different cheeses to create your own style. As Aaron always says, no matter what you use, everything will be fantastic!

KIMCHI GRILLED CHEESE

Grilled Cheese Sandwich with Stir-Fried Kimchi

PREP TIME: **3 minutes** // COOK TIME: **10 minutes** // MAKES: **2**

I don't know who first had the genius idea to add kimchi to grilled cheese. It's obvious that kimchi and cheese are an amazing combination. However, many people missed one important detail: the best kimchi for pairing with cheese isn't fresh kimchi but fried kimchi. If you're reading this, you're in luck because now you're about to experience a kimchi grilled cheese that is dramatically more delicious than any you might find online.

---

1 tbsp neutral-tasting oil
¼ yellow onion, finely diced
5 oz (150g) well-fermented kimchi, cut into small pieces (see note)
3 tbsp kimchi juice
3 tbsp unsalted butter
4 slices white bread or sourdough bread
4–8 slices American cheese (or other cheese of choice)

1. In a small pan, heat the oil over medium heat. Once nice and hot, add the onion and kimchi. Sauté for 2 minutes. Add the kimchi juice and sauté for 4 to 5 minutes or until the kimchi is caramelized and most of the liquid has evaporated. Once the kimchi is cooked through, remove it from the heat and set aside.
2. Butter one side of each slice of bread. Place half the bread butter-side down in a cold large pan. Layer on the cheese and kimchi. Close the sandwich with the other half of the bread, butter-side up.
3. Heat the pan over medium heat and cook for 2 to 4 minutes or until the bottom is golden brown and crispy. Flip the sandwich and toast the other side until it's golden brown and the cheese is fully melted.
4. Remove from the pan and slice diagonally. Enjoy!

NOTE: Well-fermented kimchi is the key to this recipe, so if your kimchi is freshly made, please wait until it tastes a little bit sour.

CREAMY PASTA WITH KIMCHI

Creamy Pasta with Kimchi

PREP TIME: **10 minutes** // COOK TIME: **15 minutes** // SERVES: **2**

If you've already tried making kimchi grilled cheese, you probably understand just how well kimchi pairs with cheese. Now it's time to take it to the next phase. A creamy, cheesy sauce with a little spicy kick and tanginess from the kimchi—it will be the combination you've been dreaming of your whole life.

½ cup (100g) well-fermented napa cabbage kimchi, finely chopped (see note)
1 tbsp Korean chili pepper flakes (gochugaru)
1 tbsp soy sauce
1 tbsp oyster sauce
1 tsp granulated sugar
Kosher salt, to taste
8.8 oz (250g) rigatoni or fettuccine
1 tbsp olive oil
½ yellow onion, thinly sliced
2–3 green onions, thinly sliced, white and green parts divided
3 white button mushrooms, finely chopped
2 strips uncooked bacon, thinly sliced
1¼ cups heavy cream
1 cup Parmigiano-Reggiano cheese, grated, plus more to serve
Freshly cracked black pepper, to serve

1. In a small bowl, stir together the kimchi, Korean chili pepper flakes, soy sauce, oyster sauce, and sugar until thoroughly combined. Set aside.
2. Bring a pot of salted water to a boil. Add the pasta and cook according to the package instructions or until al dente. Once the pasta is cooked, reserve ½ cup pasta water and drain the pasta.
3. While the pasta is cooking, to a large pan or skillet over medium-high heat, add the olive oil. Once it's nice and hot, add the yellow onion and white parts of the green onions. Sauté for 2 minutes or until fragrant.
4. Add the mushrooms and bacon. Sauté for 2 minutes or until they start to become brown. Add the seasoned kimchi and sauté for 3 minutes or until most of the liquid has evaporated.
5. Reduce the heat to medium, add the heavy cream, and simmer for 2 to 3 minutes or until the sauce gets thicker. Reduce the heat to low and add the Parmigiano-Reggiano. Stir until everything is well combined. Taste and season with salt, if needed.
6. Add the drained pasta to the pan and toss to coat. Increase the heat to medium-high and add ¼ cup of the reserved pasta water. Toss together vigorously until the pasta is evenly coated with a beautiful, glossy, emulsified sauce. (If the sauce is too thick, you can add more pasta water.)
7. Plate and top with freshly cracked black pepper, the green parts of the green onions, and more Parmigiano-Reggiano. Serve and enjoy immediately.

NOTE: Well-fermented kimchi is the key to this recipe, so if your kimchi is freshly made, please wait until it tastes a little bit sour.

CLAIRE SAYS:

If you want the sauce to be even smoother, like the ones you find in fancy restaurants, you can blend the sauce with a hand blender in Step 5.

CLAIRE SAYS:

When I was in the US, my absolute favorite dish was fettuccine Alfredo. So, whenever Aaron made this dish for me, it was usually with fettuccine, and the original name of this recipe was actually "Gochujang Fettuccine Alfredo." But when Aaron was filming the video for this recipe, he suddenly switched the pasta to pappardelle. (He said he had a spark of inspiration...) Since then, I've completely fallen for pappardelle and can't go back to fettuccine. It pairs so perfectly with this sauce, and I really hope you give it a try too!

CREAMY GOCHUJANG ALFREDO

Alfredo Pasta with Creamy Gochujang Sauce

PREP TIME: **10 minutes** // COOK TIME: **15 minutes** // SERVES: **2**

When I make fusion dishes, I often joke about feeling sorry for my Italian friends. But with this dish, I feel absolutely no guilt. This pasta combines the essence of traditional Italian pasta, the flavors of Italian-American pasta, and Korea's signature spicy kick. It's a dish that has received high praise and approval from many Italians. So stop worrying, serve this dish confidently to your Italian friends, and watch them fall in love with it!

Kosher salt, to taste
6 oz (180g) pappardelle or fettuccine
3 tbsp unsalted butter
5 garlic cloves, finely chopped
2–3 green onions, thinly sliced, white and green parts divided
1¼ cups heavy cream
1 cup Parmigiano-Reggiano cheese, grated, plus more to serve
Freshly cracked black pepper, to serve

FOR THE SEASONING PASTE

1 tbsp Korean chili paste (gochujang)
½ tbsp Korean chili pepper flakes (gochugaru)
1 tbsp oyster sauce

1. To make the seasoning paste, in a small bowl, combine all the ingredients. Mix until thoroughly combined and set aside.
2. Bring a pot of salted water to a boil. Add the pasta and cook according to the package instructions or until al dente. Once the pasta is cooked, reserve ¼ cup pasta water and drain the pasta.
3. While the pasta is cooking, to a large pan or skillet over medium-low heat, add the butter. Once the butter is melted, add the garlic and white parts of the green onions. Sauté for 2 minutes or until they start to brown.
4. Add the seasoning paste and sauté for 2 minutes or until you can see the beautiful chili oil on the surface. Add the heavy cream and reserved pasta water and stir. Gently simmer the sauce for another 2 to 3 minutes or until the sauce gets a little bit thicker. Add the Parmigiano-Reggiano and stir until everything is fully combined.
5. Add the drained pasta to the pan. Toss together vigorously until the pasta is evenly coated with a beautiful, glossy, emulsified sauce. (If the sauce is too thick, you can add more pasta water.)
6. Turn the heat off. Taste and add some salt if needed. Plate and top with freshly cracked black pepper, the green parts of the green onions, and more Parmigiano-Reggiano. Enjoy immediately.

GOCHUJANG DUBU DEOPBAP

Gochujang Tofu Rice

PREP TIME: **15 minutes** // COOK TIME: **15 minutes** // SERVES: **3**

What do you think of tofu? Flavorless? Boring? If that's what you think, I'm sure you've tried tofu cooked the wrong way. But don't worry about it. With the gochujang that's been sitting in the back of your fridge, your bland tofu will become an umami bomb.

---

1 head broccoli, cut into bite-sized pieces
½ cup potato starch (or cornstarch)
18 oz (520g) firm tofu, cut into 1-inch (2.5cm) cubes and patted dry
4 tbsp neutral-tasting oil, divided
5 garlic cloves, finely chopped
2 green onions, thinly sliced, white and green parts divided
½ tsp freshly grated ginger
½ tbsp toasted sesame oil
3 cups hot cooked rice, about 7½ oz (210g) for each serving
3 soft-boiled eggs (optional), to serve
2 mild chili peppers (1 red and 1 green) (optional), thinly sliced, to garnish
Toasted sesame seeds, to garnish

FOR THE GOCHUJANG SAUCE

2 tbsp Korean chili pepper paste (gochujang)
1 tbsp Korean chili pepper flakes (gochugaru)
1 tbsp soy sauce
1 tbsp oyster sauce
1 tsp chicken bouillon powder
1 tbsp granulated sugar
1 tbsp honey or light corn syrup
2 tbsp mirin
Freshly cracked black pepper, to taste
½ cup water
½ tbsp cornstarch

FOR THE BROCCOLI SEASONING

1 tsp minced garlic
1 tsp soy sauce
1 tbsp toasted sesame oil
1 tbsp toasted sesame seeds
Kosher salt, to taste

1. To prepare the gochujang sauce, in a small bowl, whisk together all the ingredients until thoroughly combined. Set aside.
2. In a medium pot, place a steamer basket with some water (about 3 cups) and bring to a boil. Once it comes to a boil, add the broccoli. Cover and steam for 3 to 4 minutes or until they've reached your desired doneness. Shock them in cold water and drain.
3. To a large bowl, add the drained broccoli along with all the ingredients for the broccoli seasoning and gently toss together. Taste and add salt, if needed. Set aside.
4. To a baking sheet or tray, add the potato starch. Add in the tofu and gently toss until thoroughly coated.
5. In a large pan, heat 3 tablespoons of oil over medium heat. Once it gets nice and hot, add the tofu pieces and fry for 6 to 7 minutes, flipping every few minutes, until the tofu is light golden brown and crispy on every side. (Work in batches so you don't overcrowd the pan.) Remove the tofu from the pan and set aside.
6. Place the same pan over medium-high heat. Add 1 tablespoon of oil. Once it gets nice and hot, add the garlic, white parts of the green onions, and ginger. Sauté for 1 minute or until fragrant.
7. Pour in the gochujang sauce and boil for 2 to 3 minutes. Once the sauce thickens, add the fried tofu and stir for 1 minute or until the tofu is thoroughly coated. Turn the heat off. Drizzle in the sesame oil and gently toss together.
8. To serve, divide the rice evenly between three serving plates or bowls. Add a generous amount of tofu and broccoli. Top with the soft-boiled eggs (if using). Garnish with the green parts of the green onions, chili peppers (if using), and sesame seeds. Enjoy!

CLAIRE SAYS:

I totally understand why people don't like tofu dishes. If you've tried tofu dishes several times but it's still not your thing, then trust this gochujang version and give it just one more shot. It may just break your invisible barrier and help you to start enjoying tofu.

CLAIRE SAYS:

I love this peanut butter noodle recipe as is, but if you're a fan of cilantro, you can garnish this dish with some chopped cilantro. Aaron prefers that version, but… honestly, you know… let me stop here…

PEANUT BUTTER NOODLES

Stir-Fried Noodles with Peanut Butter Sauce

PREP TIME: **10 minutes** // COOK TIME: **10 minutes** // SERVES: **2**

This is yet another incredibly simple noodle dish. Creamy, savory, mildly spicy, and bursting with rich peanut butter flavor, this dish is ready in just 20 minutes with minimal effort, so it's perfect for any day of the week. Trust me. These peanut butter noodles will truly change your life.

---

2 servings jjajangmyeon noodles (or spaghetti, udon noodles, etc.)
1 tbsp neutral-tasting oil
2 green onions, thinly sliced, white and green parts divided
3 garlic cloves, finely chopped
½ tsp freshly grated ginger
½ English cucumber, cut into thin matchsticks
2 tbsp roasted peanuts, crushed

FOR THE SAUCE

3 tbsp creamy peanut butter
1 tbsp soy sauce
1 tbsp oyster sauce
½ tbsp chicken bouillon powder
1 tbsp white vinegar
1 tsp granulated sugar
1 tbsp Korean chili pepper flakes (gochugaru)
1 tbsp toasted sesame oil

1. To make the sauce, in a small bowl, combine all the ingredients. Mix until thoroughly combined and set aside.
2. Bring a pot of water to a boil. Once boiling, cook the noodles according to the package instructions. Once the noodles are cooked, reserve 1 cup of noodle cooking water and drain the noodles. The starch from the reserved noodle cooking water will help make the sauce creamier and coat the noodles well.
3. Meanwhile, in a large wok or pan, heat the oil over medium-low heat. Once it gets nice and hot, add the white parts of the green onions, garlic, and ginger. Sauté for 1 minute or until they start to become brown and fragrant.
4. Add the sauce into the pan and stir for 1 minute or until everything is well mixed and fragrant. Add ¼ cup of reserved noodle cooking water and simmer for 1 to 2 minutes or until the sauce thickens a bit.
5. Add the drained noodles to the pan. Stir-fry for 1 minute or until everything is fully coated. Add another ¼ cup of reserved noodle cooking water to help thin out the sauce and toss for another 1 to 2 minutes. Add more noodle cooking water, if needed, to achieve your desired consistency.
6. Divide the noodles evenly between two serving plates. Top with the green parts of the green onions, cucumber, and peanuts. Serve and enjoy immediately!

BULGOGI BOKKEUMMYEON

Beef Bulgogi Noodles

PREP TIME: **15 minutes** // COOK TIME: **10 minutes** // SERVES: **2**

Do you like bulgogi (the iconic Korean BBQ beef)? How about noodles? They are both amazing, right? So, I combined them! And this proved to be the best combo in history. What are you waiting for? Let's dive right into it!

---

2 servings udon noodles (or spaghetti noodles)
1 tbsp neutral-tasting oil
2 green onions, thinly sliced, white and green parts divided
11 oz (300g) pre-sliced beef (bulgogi cut) or ribeye or tenderloin, thinly sliced (see note)
½ yellow onion, thinly sliced
4 white button mushrooms, thinly sliced
⅓ carrot (60g), cut into thin matchsticks
½ tsp dark soy sauce (optional)
½ oz (15g) garlic chives, cut into 2-inch (5cm) pieces
1 tsp toasted sesame oil
Toasted sesame seeds, to garnish

FOR THE BULGOGI SAUCE

2 tbsp soy sauce
1½ tbsp oyster sauce
2 tbsp mirin
1 tbsp granulated sugar
1 tbsp minced garlic
½ tbsp toasted sesame oil
Freshly cracked black pepper, to taste

1. To make the bulgogi sauce, in a small bowl, combine all the ingredients. Mix until thoroughly combined and set aside.
2. Bring a pot of water to a boil. Once boiling, cook the noodles according to the package instructions. Once they are cooked through, take them out and set aside.
3. In a large wok or pan, heat the oil over medium heat. Once it gets nice and hot, add the white parts of the green onions and cook for 30 seconds or until fragrant. Increase the heat to medium-high, add the beef, and cook for 2 to 3 minutes or until the beef is halfway cooked.
4. Add the onion, mushrooms, and carrot. Stir-fry for 1 to 2 minutes or until the vegetables are slightly cooked. Increase the heat to high, add the drained noodles, sauce, and dark soy sauce (if using). Toss together for 2 to 3 minutes or until the noodles are thoroughly coated with the sauce. Turn the heat off.
5. Add the garlic chives and sesame oil. Give a final mix.
6. Divide the noodles evenly between two serving plates. Top with the green parts of the green onions and sesame seeds. Serve and enjoy immediately.

NOTE: If you can't get thinly sliced beef, place a chunk of meat in a resealable plastic bag and freeze it for about 30 minutes. Once it's firm but not fully frozen, slice it thinly against the grain.

CLAIRE SAYS:

Bulgogi and cheese are a match made in heaven. If you love cheese, finish with some grated Parmigiano-Reggiano on top. It will elevate the flavors to a whole new level!

CLAIRE SAYS:

If you are using pork instead of beef, I recommend adding some grated ginger (2 teaspoons) in Step 2. As Aaron always says, pork and ginger are a fantastic duo. Do you want to know a little secret? Unlike Aaron, I prefer the one with pork. That's why I can give you this pro tip. Sorry, Aaron.

GOCHUJANG BOKKEUMMYEON

Gochujang Garlic Noodles

PREP TIME: **15 minutes** // COOK TIME: **10 minutes** // SERVES: **2**

Bibim Guksu (spicy Korean cold noodles) is probably the first dish that comes to your mind when you think of a noodle dish made with gochujang. But don't you get tired of that? Don't you want something different? Don't worry about it. These new-style gochujang noodles that are warm and full of umami will take you to a whole new gochujang world.

---

2 tbsp neutral-tasting oil
9 oz (250g) ground beef
7 garlic cloves, finely chopped
2 green onions, thinly sliced, white and green parts divided
2 servings frozen wheat noodles (or spaghetti, udon noodles, etc.)
2 baby bok choy, halved or quartered lengthwise
Generous pinch of toasted sesame seeds, to garnish
2 soft-boiled eggs (optional), to serve

FOR THE SEASONING PASTE

2 tbsp Korean chili pepper flakes (gochugaru)
1 tbsp granulated sugar
1 tbsp soy sauce
½ tbsp oyster sauce
1 tbsp mirin
1 tbsp Korean soybean paste (doenjang)
2 tbsp Korean chili paste (gochujang)

1. To make the seasoning paste, in a small bowl, combine all the ingredients. Mix until thoroughly combined and set aside.
2. In a large wok or pan, heat the oil over medium-high heat. Once hot, add the ground beef. Break up the beef and render out the fat for 2 minutes. Add the garlic and white parts of the green onions. Sauté for 2 minutes or until fragrant.
3. Reduce the heat to low. Add the seasoning paste. Give a stir for 2 more minutes or until you can see the beautiful chili oil on the surface. Be careful not to burn it. Turn off the heat.
4. Meanwhile, cook the noodles in a pot of water according to the package instructions. Once the noodles are cooked through, take them out (but leave the water in the pan), rinse under cold water, and set aside. Reserve ½ cup of noodle cooking water for later.
5. In the same water, blanch the baby bok choy for 1 minute. Drain and set aside.
6. Add the reserved noodle cooking water to the wok or pan and bring to a boil over high heat. As soon as it begins to bubble, add the drained noodles and toss together for 1 minute or until the noodles are completely coated.
7. Divide the noodles evenly between two serving plates. Top with the baby bok choy, the green parts of the green onions, sesame seeds, and soft-boiled eggs (if using). Enjoy!

GALBIJJIM BOURGUIGNON

Korean-Style Beef Bourguignon

PREP TIME: **30 minutes** // COOK TIME: **2 hours** // SERVES: **4**

This isn't exactly a classic boeuf bourguignon. It's a delightful fusion of Western cooking techniques inspired by bourguignon and the incredible flavors of galbijjim (Korean braised short ribs). I decided to call it galbijjim bourguignon. And this incredibly tender, succulent, and flavorful braised beef is sure to become your staple for special occasions, just like traditional galbijjim.

---

4 tbsp neutral-tasting oil, divided
2½ lb (1.2kg) chuck flap tail or boneless short ribs, cut into 2-inch (5cm) cubes and patted dry
8½ cups + 1 tbsp water, divided, plus more if needed
½ large yellow onion, roughly chopped
4 green onions, cut into 2-inch (5cm) pieces, plus more to garnish
1 red apple, cut into large pieces
9 oz (250g) Korean radish or daikon, peeled and cut into large cubes
7 oz (200g) large carrot, peeled and cut into large cubes
5 shiitake mushrooms, quartered (see note)
1 mild red chili pepper (optional), thinly sliced diagonally
5 shishito peppers (optional), cut diagonally into 2-inch (5cm) pieces
½ tbsp cornstarch

FOR THE MASHED POTATOES

5 Yukon Gold potatoes, peeled and diced
3 tbsp unsalted butter
Generous pinch of kosher salt

FOR THE GALBIJJIM SAUCE

½ cup soy sauce
2 tbsp oyster sauce
3 tbsp granulated sugar
½ tbsp Korean beef stock powder (Dasida) or chicken bouillon powder
2 tbsp mirin
2 tbsp minced garlic
2 tbsp toasted sesame oil
2 tbsp light corn syrup
Freshly cracked black pepper, to taste

1. To make the galbijjim sauce, in a small bowl, combine all the ingredients. Mix until thoroughly combined and set aside.
2. To a large pan or skillet, add 2 tablespoons of oil and heat it over high heat. Once it gets nice and hot, add half the beef pieces and sear for 3 to 4 minutes or until nicely browned on both sides. Take them out and repeat with the remaining beef pieces. Set aside.
3. To a stock pot, add 8 cups of water, along with the yellow onion, green onions, apple, and galbijjim sauce. Bring to a boil. Once it comes to a boil, reduce the heat to medium and add the beef. Cover and simmer for an hour.
4. Meanwhile, to prepare the mashed potatoes, bring a pot of water to a boil. Once it comes to a boil, reduce the heat to low. Add the potatoes and cook for 25 minutes or until cooked through.
5. Drain the potatoes. Add the butter and a generous pinch of salt. Mash the potatoes to your desired consistency. Keep warm and set aside.
6. Using a strainer, remove the onion and apple from the stock pot. Press to squeeze out as much liquid as possible, and discard the solids. Reduce the heat to medium-low. Cover and simmer for 30 more minutes or until the beef is falling apart tender. (If the meat hasn't reached your desired doneness, add some more water and cook a little bit longer.)
7. Once the beef is tender, reduce the heat to low. Add the radish and stir. Cover and simmer for 10 minutes or until it starts to become translucent. Add the carrot, mushrooms, and ½ cup of water. Cook for 10 more minutes or until the carrot gets tender.
8. Add the chili peppers (if using) and give a final mix. Turn the heat off.
9. Scoop out 1 cup of the braising liquid and add it to a saucepan. Bring to a boil. When it starts to bubble, in a small bowl, mix the cornstarch with the remaining 1 tablespoon of water to create a slurry. Add the slurry to the sauce and immediately stir until the sauce is thickened and shiny, about 1 minute. Remove from the heat and set aside.

CLAIRE SAYS:

Galbijjim is supposed to be eaten with your hands like a caveperson. Even if it's a fancy dish, that's the vibe. But if you don't want to dirty your hands or you just want to enjoy it gracefully but still want some galbijjim, this is it. This is the way to go.

10. To assemble each serving, take a spoonful of mashed potatoes and place on a serving plate. Top with galbijjim bourguignon. Drizzle on the desired amount of gravy sauce and sprinkle with sliced green onions. Enjoy!

NOTE: For a more beautiful presentation, carve a little star on the surface of two of the mushrooms. They will make it look fancier.

KOREAN FRIED CHICKEN SANDWICH

Chicken Sandwich with Korean Sweet and Spicy Sauce

PREP TIME: **35 minutes + 1 hour to brine** // COOK TIME: **20 minutes** // SERVES: **5**

I do love sandwiches, especially chicken sandwiches. So, I always wondered what it would be like to make a chicken sandwich using the king of fried chicken: Korean fried chicken. That's how this recipe came to be. And one of my subscribers said that this is the best chicken sandwich they've ever eaten, hands down, no contenders.

CLAIRE SAYS:

Brining may seem intimidating, but if you've decided to make this, I would never skip it. This step is essential for achieving juicy and tender Korean fried chicken. So please give it a try. If you do, you will meet one of the best chicken sandwiches you've ever had.

5 large boneless, skinless chicken thighs or breasts, about 1.3 lb (600g) in total
3 cups (450g) Korean fried chicken powder mix (or potato starch, cornstarch), divided
1 cup cold water
High-heat oil (such as canola, avocado, vegetable, etc.), for frying
5 sandwich buns
4 tbsp unsalted butter, softened
5 pickled cucumbers or dill pickles, sliced lengthwise

FOR THE BRINE

3 cups water
½ tbsp kosher salt
1 tbsp granulated sugar
1 tbsp chicken bouillon powder
1 tbsp garlic powder
1 tbsp onion powder
½ tbsp cayenne pepper
1 tbsp white vinegar
½ tsp freshly cracked black pepper

FOR THE COLESLAW

4 cups green cabbage, thinly sliced
2 oz (60g) carrot, thinly sliced
1 green onion, thinly sliced
⅓ cup Korean pickled radish (chicken mu) (optional), finely chopped
1 cup Kewpie mayonnaise
2 tbsp apple cider vinegar
½ tbsp granulated sugar
½ tsp kosher salt
¼ tsp freshly cracked black pepper

FOR THE KOREAN FRIED CHICKEN SAUCE

2 tbsp Korean chili paste (gochujang)
5 tbsp ketchup
2 tbsp soy sauce
2 tbsp Korean chili pepper flakes (gochugaru)
3 tbsp granulated sugar
1 tbsp minced garlic
8 tbsp light corn syrup
3 tbsp water

FOR THE MAYO SAUCE

4 tbsp Kewpie mayonnaise
1 tbsp horseradish
1 tbsp Korean fried chicken sauce

1. To prepare the brine, in a large bowl, combine all the ingredients and stir until everything is fully dissolved.
2. Add the chicken to the brine, cover with a lid or plastic wrap, and refrigerate for at least 1 hour or overnight.
3. To prepare the coleslaw, in a medium bowl, mix together all of the ingredients. Cover with plastic wrap and refrigerate until ready to use.
4. To prepare the Korean fried chicken sauce, in a saucepan, combine all the ingredients. Place over medium heat. Once it starts to bubble and the sugar is completely dissolved, remove it from the heat and set aside.
5. To prepare the mayo sauce, in a small bowl, mix all the ingredients until combined. Set aside.
6. In a large bowl, whisk together 1 cup Korean fried chicken powder mix and 1 cup cold water until thoroughly combined. For the dry batter, spread the remaining 2 cups Korean fried chicken powder mix onto a baking sheet or tray.
7. Take a piece of chicken and first coat it in the dry batter. Then, dip it into the wet batter. After that, return the chicken to the dry batter and coat it again. Be sure to gently press the batter onto the chicken to help it stick. Repeat with the remaining chicken.
8. In a large Dutch oven or heavy-bottomed pot, heat about 2 inches (5cm) of cooking oil to 340°F (170°C). Working in batches, carefully place the chicken pieces in the oil (dropping them away from you). Fry for 7 to 8 minutes or until crispy and golden brown.
9. Once the chicken is cooked through, remove from the oil and drain on a cooling rack. Dunk it in the Korean fried chicken sauce and coat well. Set aside.
10. Cut the sandwich buns in half and spread the butter generously over the cut sides of the buns. In a large dry pan, toast all of the buns cut-side down over medium heat until browned.
11. To assemble the sandwiches, on the bottom buns, spread out the mayo sauce, followed by coleslaw, sliced pickles, and a Korean fried chicken piece. Top with the top bun and enjoy.

BULGOGI BURRITO

Korean BBQ Burrito

PREP TIME: **30 minutes + making bulgogi** // COOK TIME: **None** // SERVES: **4–6**

This has been a carefully hidden secret for a long time: Mexican and Korean dishes pair surprisingly well together. I could provide countless examples to prove this, but this dish, standing as evidence #1, will convince you instantly.

4–6 flour or corn tortillas, warmed
Dajin Sogogi Bulgogi (page 93) or Dajin Dwaejigogi Bulgogi (page 94), to serve
4 lettuce leaves, thinly sliced
1 large avocado, peeled and sliced
Sour cream, to serve
Freshly grated manchego cheese, to serve

FOR THE SALSA

1 large tomato, cored and diced
¼ yellow onion, diced
1 medium jalapeño pepper, finely chopped
⅛ cup cilantro leaves, finely chopped
3 tbsp canned corn (optional)
Juice of ½ lime
Kosher salt, to taste
Freshly cracked black pepper, to taste

FOR THE CILANTRO LIME RICE

2 cups hot cooked rice, about 15 oz (420g)
Zest and juice of ½ lime
Zest of ½ lemon
½ cup cilantro leaves, finely chopped
Generous pinch of kosher salt, to taste
1 tbsp unsalted butter

1. To make the salsa, in a medium bowl, combine all the ingredients. Mix until thoroughly combined and set aside.
2. To make the cilantro lime rice, in a medium bowl, add all the ingredients and stir until thoroughly mixed or the butter is fully melted and incorporated.
3. On a warm tortilla, spread the rice evenly in the center. Top it with a generous amount of the bulgogi of your choice, salsa, lettuce, avocado, sour cream, and a grating of manchego cheese.
4. Fold the sides toward the center, then grab the bottom and roll it over the filling and the folded edges, making it nice and tight until fully wrapped. Repeat with the remaining tortillas.

CLAIRE SAYS:

This bulgogi burrito is an excellent option for meal prep. You can prepare it in advance, store it in the fridge, and enjoy it over the next few days. If you want to take it a step further, vacuum-sealing it before freezing will keep it fresh for several months.

CLAIRE SAYS:

This creamy tteokbokki is even more satisfying when made with longer, noodle-shaped rice cakes instead of the usual ones. The long, chewy rice cakes create a texture similar to noodles, making each bite incredibly enjoyable. If you can find these noodle-shaped rice cakes, I highly recommend giving them a try! You won't regret it!

ROSÉ TTEOKBOKKI

Creamy Spicy Rice Cakes

PREP TIME: **10 minutes** // COOK TIME: **20 minutes** // SERVES: **2**

If you love tteokbokki but want something a little less spicy and more creamy, this rosé tteokbokki is the perfect choice. The chewy rice cakes are smothered in a creamy sauce with just the right amount of heat, making it a delicious and satisfying twist on the classic.

---

11 oz (320g) rice cakes for tteokbokki (see note)
½ tbsp neutral-tasting oil
2–3 strips uncooked bacon, cut into bite-sized pieces
8 mini sausages, lightly scored
1 cup whole milk
1 cup heavy cream
2 hard-boiled eggs (optional), to serve
Kosher salt, to taste
1 green onion, thinly sliced, to garnish

FOR THE SEASONING PASTE

2–3 tbsp Korean chili pepper flakes (gochugaru) (see note)
½ tbsp Korean chili paste (gochujang)
2 tbsp granulated sugar
1 tbsp Korean beef stock powder (Dasida) or chicken bouillon powder
½ tbsp Korean curry powder or ¼ curry block
¼ tsp freshly cracked black pepper
3 tbsp water

1. To make the seasoning paste, in a small bowl, combine all the ingredients. Mix until thoroughly combined and set aside.
2. Bring a pot of water to a boil. Once boiling, blanch the rice cakes for 2 minutes or until they just start to soften. Take them out and set aside.
3. In a large pan or skillet, heat the oil over medium-low heat. Once it gets nice and hot, add the bacon and sausages. Cook for 2 minutes or until the fat is rendered.
4. Add the seasoning paste. Sauté for 30 seconds to 1 minute. Watch the pan carefully and stir constantly, as the chili pepper flakes can easily burn.
5. Add the milk and heavy cream. Simmer, stirring occasionally, for 4 minutes or until all the flavors come together. Be sure not to let the mixture come to a full boil.
6. Add the drained rice cakes and hard-boiled eggs (if using). Simmer, stirring occasionally, for another 5 to 6 minutes or until the sauce starts to thicken.
7. Taste and add more salt, if desired. Garnish with sliced green onion. Serve it directly from the pan or transfer it to a serving plate. Enjoy!

NOTES: If using frozen rice cakes, thaw in the fridge overnight.

If you want the sauce to have a more silky and smooth texture, I recommend using fine gochugaru (Korean chili pepper powder). To make it yourself, add regular gochugaru to a blender and blend it on high until powdered.

KIMCHI CHEESE FRIES

Crispy Fries with Stir-Fried Kimchi

PREP TIME: **20 minutes** // COOK TIME: **10 minutes** // SERVES: **2**

You already know that fries and cheese pair incredibly well with beer. But you know what? In Korean cuisine, stir-fried kimchi and bulgogi also go well with drinks. This dish beautifully combines the best of the West and the East, making it the ultimate companion for beer.

---

1 tbsp neutral-tasting oil, divided
1 cup well-fermented kimchi, chopped into small, bite-sized pieces (see note)
3 tbsp kimchi juice
15 oz (420g) frozen French fries, prepared according to package instructions
¼ red onion, finely diced
Freshly grated aged manchego cheese or Parmigiano-Reggiano, to serve
Sour cream, to serve
Nacho cheese sauce, to serve
Sriracha, to serve
Cilantro leaves (or green onions), to garnish

FOR THE BULGOGI TOPPING

4 oz (120g) ground beef
1 tbsp soy sauce
½ tbsp granulated sugar
½ tbsp mirin
½ tbsp oyster sauce
½ tbsp minced garlic
1 tsp toasted sesame oil
Freshly cracked black pepper, to taste

1. To make the bulgogi topping, in a small bowl, combine all the ingredients. Mix until thoroughly combined.
2. In a small pan or skillet, heat ½ tablespoon of oil over medium-high heat. Once it's nice and hot, add the bulgogi topping and sauté for 3 minutes or until the beef is cooked through. Set aside.
3. In another small pan, heat the remaining ½ tablespoon of oil over medium heat. Add the kimchi and kimchi juice. Cook for 4 minutes or until the kimchi is wilted down and most of the liquid has evaporated. Set aside.
4. Place the French fries on a serving plate. Top with the bulgogi topping, onion, cooked kimchi, and cheese. Drizzle generously with sour cream, nacho cheese sauce, and sriracha. Garnish with cilantro and serve. Enjoy!

NOTE: Well-fermented kimchi is the key to this recipe, so if your kimchi is freshly made, please wait until it tastes a little bit sour.

CLAIRE SAYS:

These kimchi cheese fries are the perfect snack for drinking, so make sure you have enough beer in your fridge. Otherwise, it will be torture.

JAPANESE

CLAIRE SAYS:

This Japanese potato salad is incredibly versatile and makes a perfect side dish for almost any meal. It also works great as a delicious sandwich filling, so please give it a try. You won't regret it.

POTETO SARADA

Japanese Potato Salad

PREP TIME: **20 minutes** // COOK TIME: **30 minutes** // SERVES: **6**

I've never met anyone who doesn't like potatoes. But if you're saying, "That's me," then let me start by saying I'm sorry. At the same time, I envy you because you still have the chance to fall in love with potatoes. That's right—this creamy Japanese-style potato salad, one of the most popular party foods, side dishes, and bar foods in Japan, will surely turn anyone into a potato lover in no time.

---

4 Yukon Gold or russet potatoes, about 1.3 lb (600g) in total, peeled and roughly chopped
Kosher salt, to taste
¼ yellow onion, finely diced
1 tbsp white vinegar (or rice vinegar)
1 tsp granulated sugar
Freshly cracked black pepper, to taste
½ English cucumber, cut into thin half-moon slices
½ tsp kosher salt
⅓ carrot (60g), cut into thin half-moon slices
1 large hard-boiled egg, cooled and finely chopped
3 slices ham, cut into small bite-sized pieces
3 tbsp canned corn
7 tbsp Kewpie mayonnaise

1. Add the potatoes to a medium pot and cover with water. Generously season the water with salt and bring to a boil. Once it starts to boil, reduce the heat to medium and simmer for 15 minutes or until fork-tender.
2. Transfer the potatoes to a large mixing bowl and mash, leaving some small chunks if you prefer. While the potatoes are still hot, add the onion and mix well. (The heat from the potatoes will slightly cook the onion, softening its sharpness while leaving a pleasant crunch.) Add the vinegar, sugar, salt (to taste), and pepper. Stir to combine. Set aside to cool.
3. Place the cucumber slices in a medium bowl. Add the ½ teaspoon salt and toss. Let sit for 10 minutes to draw out excess moisture. Squeeze out any excess water. Set aside.
4. Bring a pot of water to a boil and blanch the carrot slices for 2 to 3 minutes. Rinse under cold water and drain well.
5. Add the cucumber, carrot, chopped egg, ham, corn, and Kewpie mayonnaise to the potato mixture and stir everything together until thoroughly combined. (Add more mayonnaise if you like it creamier.) Give it a final taste and add more salt and pepper if needed. Serve immediately or store in an airtight container in the fridge for up to 4 days. There's no need to reheat it, as it's best enjoyed chilled.

TENSHINHAN

Crabmeat Omelet Over Rice

PREP TIME: **3 minutes** // COOK TIME: **7 minutes** // SERVES: **2**

You know those days when you're too tired to cook but still want something more satisfying than instant noodles or takeout? That's when this Japanese-style egg rice bowl comes to the rescue. It requires only a few ingredients and is insanely easy to make. In just 15 minutes, you can enjoy a warm, filling, and comforting meal in a bowl.

---

6 large eggs, beaten, divided
4 small imitation crab sticks (or cooked shrimp), torn into strips
Kosher salt, to taste
2 tbsp neutral-tasting oil, divided
2 cups hot cooked short-grain rice, about 7½ oz (210g) for each serving

FOR THE SAUCE

1 cup water
1 tbsp mirin
1 tbsp soy sauce
½ tbsp oyster sauce
1 tsp chicken bouillon powder
1 tsp granulated sugar
½ tsp toasted sesame oil
1 tbsp frozen peas
1 tbsp cornstarch
2 tbsp water

1. To make the sauce, in a small saucepan, combine all the ingredients except the cornstarch and water. Bring to a boil over medium-high heat. Meanwhile, in a small bowl, whisk together the cornstarch and water to create a slurry. Once the sauce starts to boil, add the slurry and stir until nice and thickened. Keep warm and set aside.
2. To a large bowl, add the eggs, crabmeat, and salt, and whisk together until thoroughly combined.
3. In a medium pan, add 1 tablespoon of oil and heat over medium-high heat. Once it gets nice and hot, pour in half of the egg mixture and cook for 1 to 2 minutes or until the omelet is cooked but the top is still a bit runny.
4. To serve, place 1 cup of rice on a plate or bowl. Slide the omelet over the rice and tuck the edges down. Pour half of the sauce over the omelet. Repeat the process for the second bowl. Serve immediately.

CLAIRE SAYS:

Aaron introduced this as a quick weeknight dinner for busy days, but I don't think it has to be limited to that. Warm rice, a fluffy egg omelet, and a nice, glossy, savory sauce make this dish perfect for breakfast too. If you're someone who loves eating eggs for breakfast, I highly recommend it. And here's a pro tip: using fried rice instead of plain rice will make it even more delicious. You're welcome!

CLAIRE SAYS:

I know this might not be the traditional way to enjoy gyudon. It's probably just my personal preference. But I have to say it as a taste tester: If you have Kewpie mayo at home, drizzle a little on top and mix it before taking a bite. This way, you'll experience my absolute favorite style of gyudon.

GYUDON

Beef Rice Bowl

PREP TIME: **10 minutes** // COOK TIME: **10 minutes** // SERVES: **2**

Whenever I visit Japan, I always enjoy having this dish for breakfast. Thinly sliced beef and tender onions simmered in a slightly sweet yet savory sauce, served over a warm bowl of rice—it's hard to find a more perfectly balanced breakfast than this. But can you believe that you can enjoy this satisfying meal at home in under 20 minutes? That's right, I just saved you a thousand dollars for the plane tickets to Japan. You're welcome!

---

1 yellow onion, thinly sliced
½ lb (225g) thinly sliced beef chuck or ribeye, cut into bite-sized pieces (see note)
2 cups hot cooked short-grain rice, about 7½ oz (210g) for each serving
1 soft-boiled egg, halved, divided
Japanese red pickled ginger (beni shoga) (optional), to garnish
1 green onion, thinly sliced

FOR THE SAUCE

¾ cup water
½ tsp Japanese bonito soup stock powder (Hondashi)
3 tbsp soy sauce
3 tbsp mirin
½ tbsp granulated sugar

1. In a large pan, add all the sauce ingredients and whisk together until thoroughly combined. Add the onion and bring to a boil. Once it starts to boil, reduce the heat to medium and simmer for 2 minutes or until the onion is translucent.
2. Add the beef, stir, and simmer, covered, for 5 minutes or until the beef is cooked through. (If it hasn't reached your desired tenderness, add more water and cook a little longer over low heat. The longer you simmer, the more tender it will be.) Meanwhile, if there is any scum, skim it off with a fine-mesh skimmer or ladle.
3. Divide the rice evenly between two serving bowls. Add the beef and onion on top of the rice. (Do not pour everything out all at once. It will be too salty.) Drizzle 1 or 2 tablespoons of the broth over the beef. Garnish with soft-boiled egg, pickled ginger (if using), and green onion. Serve immediately.

NOTE: If you can't get thinly sliced beef, place a chunk of meat in a resealable plastic bag and freeze it for about 30 minutes. Once it's firm but not fully frozen, slice it thinly against the grain.

TERIYAKI SAUCE

Teriyaki Sauce

PREP TIME: **3 minutes** // COOK TIME: **20 minutes** // MAKES: **1½ cups**

I could've shared a simple teriyaki chicken recipe on this page, but instead I wanted to highlight the incredible versatility of this classic Japanese sauce. This homemade teriyaki sauce is not just for teriyaki chicken; it's perfect for countless Japanese-style dishes. You can use it as a glaze for meats, fish, or tofu, or as a stir-fry sauce for vegetables or noodles. No matter how you use this, it will pair beautifully with almost anything and quickly become a staple in your kitchen.

---

4 green onions (preferably white part), cut into 2-inch (5cm) pieces
¼ yellow onion
4 garlic cloves
½ oz (15g) fresh ginger, peeled
1 cup soy sauce
1 cup mirin (see note)
½ cup sake (see note)
½ cup granulated sugar

1. Preheat the broiler.
2. Place the green onions, yellow onion, garlic, and ginger on a baking sheet and broil for 10 minutes or until charred on the surface. (You can also use a blowtorch.)
3. In a small saucepan, combine the soy sauce, mirin, sake, and sugar until thoroughly combined. Add the charred vegetables and bring to a boil. Once it comes to a boil, reduce the heat to low and simmer, stirring occasionally, for 10 more minutes or until the sauce is reduced by two thirds. Remove from the heat.
4. Once completely cooled, strain the mixture into a jar or bottle through a strainer and discard the solids. Use immediately or store in the fridge for up to 3 months.

NOTE: In this recipe, mirin and sake cannot be substituted with other cooking wines.

CLAIRE SAYS:

The balance of salty and sweet in this aromatic teriyaki sauce is truly remarkable—there's really no comparison to store-bought versions. I really hope you give it a try. You can find our teriyaki chicken recipe using this sauce on our YouTube channel and blog. Personally, I'm a huge fan of using this sauce to make yaki udon—it's absolutely delicious!

CLAIRE SAYS:

If deep-frying feels a bit intimidating, shallow-frying is absolutely fine. Just make sure to increase the cooking time slightly or cook until the internal temperature reaches 165°F (75°C). And for your information, Aaron has actually been eating katsu once a week for the past few years.

CHICKEN KATSU

Japanese Chicken Cutlet

PREP TIME: **20 minutes** // COOK TIME: **15 minutes** // SERVES: **4**

Would you believe me if I said I've been eating this dish at least once a week, or at the very least, every two weeks, for most of my life? From childhood to now, I've never once thought I was tired of it, and I don't think that will ever happen in the future. (Okay, I might be exaggerating—I probably skipped a few weeks during my time as a Navy officer.) From kids to elders, all over the world, everyone seems to love this crispy Japanese fried chicken with a sweet and tangy sauce. While pork is a more classic choice for katsu, I included this chicken version in the book so more people can enjoy it.

---

4 boneless, skinless chicken breasts
Kosher salt, to taste
Freshly cracked black pepper, to taste
1½ cups all-purpose flour
2 large eggs
2 cups panko breadcrumbs
High-heat oil (such as canola, avocado, vegetable, etc.), for frying
4 cups hot cooked short-grain rice, about 7½ oz (210g) for each serving
4 cups shredded green cabbage (optional), soaked in cold water and drained, to serve
Cherry tomatoes (optional), to serve

FOR THE KATSU SAUCE

6 tbsp ketchup
1 tbsp soy sauce
½ tbsp oyster sauce
2 tbsp Worcestershire sauce
1 tbsp granulated sugar

FOR THE SESAME DRESSING (OPTIONAL)

3 tbsp toasted sesame seeds, ground
1 tbsp granulated sugar
5 tbsp Kewpie mayonnaise
1 tbsp white vinegar (or rice vinegar)
1 tsp soy sauce
½ tbsp toasted sesame oil
Kosher salt, to taste

1. To prepare the katsu sauce, in a small bowl, whisk together all the ingredients until thoroughly combined. Set aside.
2. To make the sesame dressing (if using with the cabbage), in a small bowl, whisk together all the ingredients until thoroughly combined. Set aside.
3. Place a chicken breast in a sealable plastic bag and pound it out with a meat mallet until even in thickness throughout. Lightly season both sides with salt and pepper. Repeat with the remaining chicken pieces. Set aside.
4. Prepare three separate bowls or trays for the breading station. To the first, add the all-purpose flour. In the second, beat the eggs until well mixed. And to the third, add the panko breadcrumbs.
5. Evenly coat a piece of chicken in the flour and shake off any excess. Thoroughly coat the chicken in the egg wash. Make sure there are no dry spots. Lastly, cover with a good amount of breadcrumbs and press it down so that they can stick to the surface. Repeat with the remaining chicken pieces. Set aside.
6. In a large Dutch oven or heavy-bottomed pot, heat about 2 inches (5cm) of cooking oil to 340°F (170°C). Working two at a time, carefully place the chicken pieces in the oil. Fry for 6 to 8 minutes or until crispy golden brown and cooked through. Remove from the hot oil and let rest on a wire rack. Repeat with the remaining chicken.
7. To serve, place the rice, cabbage (if using) with sesame dressing, and cherry tomatoes (if using) on serving plates. Cut the chicken katsu into ½-inch (1.25cm) pieces and plate. Serve immediately with the katsu sauce on the side.

NOTE: You can store leftovers in an airtight container. Keep them in the fridge for up to 2 days or in the freezer for up to a month. You can reheat them in the oven or air fryer.

KATSUDON

Chicken Cutlet Rice Bowl

PREP TIME: **5 minutes + making Chicken Katsu** // COOK TIME: **10 minutes** // SERVES: **2**

The Japanese have crafted the art of creating a simple yet perfect meal with donburi (Japanese-style rice bowls). Among them, this dish—with freshly cooked rice topped with fluffy eggs and ultra-crispy chicken katsu—truly deserves to be called the king of donburi.

---

2 pieces Chicken Katsu (page 139), cut into ½-inch (1.25cm) pieces
½ yellow onion, thinly sliced, divided
4 large eggs, beaten, divided
2 cups hot cooked short-grain rice, about 7½ oz (210g) for each serving
2 green onions, thinly sliced, divided, to garnish
Japanese parsley (mitsuba) (optional), roughly chopped, to garnish
Japanese seven spice (shichimi togarashi) (optional), to serve

FOR THE KATSUDON SAUCE

1 cup water
½ tsp Japanese bonito soup stock powder (Hondashi)
3 tbsp soy sauce
3 tbsp mirin
½ tbsp granulated sugar

1. To prepare the katsudon sauce, in a small bowl, whisk together all the ingredients until thoroughly combined.
2. In a small pan, add half of the sauce and half of the onion and bring to a boil. (Make sure to cook one serving at a time. This seems like a hassle, but it gives you a better result in the end.)
3. Once the onion is soft and translucent, reduce the heat to medium. Carefully add the chicken katsu and simmer for 30 seconds or until only the bottom part soaks up the sauce. Remove the katsu from the sauce and set aside.
4. To the pan, add half of the beaten eggs and cook for 1 to 2 minutes or until your desired doneness. Shake your pan a bit so that nothing gets stuck on the bottom. (Do not overcook the eggs because the residual heat and the heat from the rice will cook them more later.)
5. To assemble, add half the rice to a serving bowl. Gently pour the egg mixture over the rice. Top with the katsu, green onion, and mitsuba (if using). Repeat with the remaining ingredients. Serve with Japanese seven spice (if using).

CLAIRE SAYS:

This katsudon recipe is tailored for our family, and we love for the cutlets to stay crispy. If you prefer the classic version, where the flavorful sauce soaks into the entire cutlet, simply skip removing the cutlet in Step 3 and follow the rest of the recipe as is.

CLAIRE SAYS:

The combination of this super creamy and velvety Japanese curry with the ultimate crispy katsu might just be one of the greatest pairings in history. While I love eating katsu with katsu sauce, I personally prefer this combination more.

KATSU CURRY

Japanese Curry with Chicken Cutlet

PREP TIME: **10 minutes + making Chicken Katsu** // COOK TIME: **90 minutes** // SERVES: **10**

There's so much I could say about this recipe, but I'll let one of our lovely subscribers' comments speak for me instead: "I cannot tell you how many times I have made this exact recipe over the last couple of years after watching this video. I cook this for family, friends, whoever will eat my cooking ... I've only gotten compliments, and I've had more than one person ask me for the recipe. I just sent them this video! Thank you!"

---

4 tbsp neutral-tasting oil, divided
4 large yellow onions, thinly sliced
7 oz (200g) carrot, roughly chopped
3 Yukon Gold potatoes, roughly chopped
3 tbsp tomato paste
1 tbsp cumin powder
8 cups water
1½ tbsp chicken bouillon powder
1 tbsp soy sauce
1 tbsp Worcestershire sauce
1 (8 oz/220g) package store-bought Japanese curry roux
2 tbsp unsalted butter
10 cups hot cooked rice, about 7½ oz (210g) for each serving
10 pieces Chicken Katsu (page 139), cut into ½-inch (1.25cm) pieces
Green onions, thinly sliced (optional), to garnish
Pickled scallions (optional), to garnish
Japanese red pickled ginger (beni shoga) (optional), to garnish

1. In a large heavy-bottomed pot, heat 3 tablespoons of oil over medium heat. Once it gets nice and hot, add the onions and sauté for 40 minutes or until deeply caramelized.
2. Meanwhile, in another large pan, heat 1 tablespoon of oil over medium heat. Once it gets nice and hot, add the carrot and potatoes and cook for 10 minutes or until golden brown. Set aside.
3. Once the onions are deeply caramelized, add the tomato paste and cumin powder. Stir together for 1 minute or until thoroughly mixed. Add the water, chicken bouillon powder, soy sauce, Worcestershire sauce, potatoes, and carrot, and stir to combine. Simmer, covered, for 30 minutes over medium-low heat.
4. Turn off the heat. Add the Japanese curry roux and unsalted butter and stir until well combined. Using an immersion blender, blend on high speed until as smooth as possible. (If you use a normal blender, make sure to cool down the curry before blending.)
5. Gently heat the curry over medium heat until it starts to boil. Remove from the heat and keep warm until ready to serve.
6. To serve, plate 1 cup of hot cooked rice on a plate. Pour in some curry around the rice. Place the sliced chicken katsu on top of the curry. Garnish with some green onions, pickled scallions, and red pickled ginger, if using. Serve immediately.

NOTE: You can store leftovers in an airtight container. Keep them in the fridge for up to 3 days or in the freezer for up to a month. You can reheat them in the microwave or on the stovetop.

OKONOMIYAKI

Savory Cabbage Pancakes

PREP TIME: **10 minutes** // COOK TIME: **25 minutes** // MAKES: **2**

Okonomiyaki, which translates to "grill what you like," is Japan's iconic savory pancake. It's not only incredibly delicious but also a hugely popular street food. I won't go into detail about the taste, as that speaks for itself. What I've always loved the most is the meaning behind its name. It highlights how adaptable this dish is and perfectly aligns with my philosophy: "Don't worry about it. Just use what you have." I'm sure many of you feel the same way right now. So, go check your fridge and enjoy making your own customized version of okonomiyaki!

---

7 oz (200g) green cabbage, cut into small, bite-sized pieces
2 green onions, thinly sliced
5 peeled and deveined shrimp, blanched, cut into small, bite-sized pieces
0.7 oz (20g) Japanese red pickled ginger (beni shoga), roughly chopped
1 oz (30g) tempura scraps (tenkasu) (optional)
2 tsp neutral-tasting oil, to coat, divided
6 slices (4 oz/110g) thinly sliced pork belly, cut into 4-inch (10cm) pieces
Kewpie mayonnaise, to serve
Dried green seaweed (aonori) (optional), to serve
Dried bonito flakes, to serve

FOR THE OKONOMIYAKI SAUCE

6 tbsp Worcestershire sauce
6 tbsp ketchup
2 tbsp granulated sugar

FOR THE BATTER

½ cup cold water
½ tsp Japanese bonito soup stock powder (Hondashi)
1 cup all-purpose flour
¼ tsp kosher salt
¼ tsp baking powder
1 tbsp cornstarch
2 large eggs

1. To make the okonomiyaki sauce, in a saucepan, stir together all the ingredients until fully combined. Bring to a boil over low heat. Once it comes to a boil and starts to thicken, remove from the heat and let cool completely. Set aside.
2. To make the batter, in a small bowl, stir together the cold water and Japanese bonito soup stock powder to make dashi broth. In a large mixing bowl, whisk together the flour, salt, baking powder, and cornstarch. Crack the eggs into the bowl, add the dashi broth, and whisk everything together. Do not over-stir it.
3. Add the cabbage, green onions, shrimp, pickled ginger, and tempura scraps (if using) to the batter and mix with a spatula.
4. To a medium nonstick pan, add 1 teaspoon of oil. Coat the bottom of the pan with a light layer of the oil using a folded paper towel. Heat over low heat. Once it gets nice and hot, add half of the batter and make it into a 1-inch (2.5cm) thick circle. Top with half of the pork belly. Cover and slowly cook for 3 to 4 minutes.
5. Once the bottom is nicely browned, flip and cook the other side for another 2 to 3 minutes, covered.
6. When the pork belly is cooked through and turns golden brown, flip and cook for 1 more minute. Poke in the middle with a fork and check if the pancake is cooked through. Transfer to a serving plate and repeat with the remaining batter.
7. To serve, spread a good amount of okonomiyaki sauce on top with a spoon. Top with Kewpie mayonnaise, dried green seaweed (if using), and bonito flakes. Serve immediately.

CLAIRE SAYS:

Of course, you can use store-bought sauce instead of making your own okonomiyaki sauce, and that's totally fine. However, I can assure you there will definitely be a noticeable difference in flavor. Plus, this homemade sauce can be stored in a jar or sauce bottle in the fridge for about 2 weeks, so it's absolutely worth making.

CLAIRE SAYS:

The beauty of Aaron's version of miso ramen is the generous variety of toppings that provide contrasting textures. The savory, rich, porky miso-based broth combined with these varied textures creates an incredibly satisfying experience that's hard to put into words.

MISO RAMEN

Japanese Soybean Paste Ramen

PREP TIME: **15 minutes** // COOK TIME: **15 minutes + 10 minutes for the chashu (optional)** // SERVES: **2**

It seems like too many people feel overwhelmed when it comes to making ramen. Sure, there are some types of ramen where making the broth alone can take over a day. But, as always, you don't have to worry about it. This miso ramen will be proof number one that you can easily make delicious ramen at home—even better than what you'd get at a restaurant.

2½ tbsp lard (or neutral-tasting oil), divided
3 green onions, thinly sliced, white and green parts divided
3½ oz (100g) mung bean sprouts
2 servings cooked ramen noodles
2 soft-boiled eggs, halved, to serve
2 tbsp canned corn, to serve
Dried seaweed (optional), to serve

FOR THE BROTH

4 cups water
1 tbsp chicken bouillon powder
1 tsp Japanese bonito soup stock powder (Hondashi)
1 tbsp minced garlic
½ tsp freshly grated ginger
5 oz (150g) ground pork
¼ tsp white pepper (or black pepper)
1 tbsp mirin
2 tsp granulated sugar
4 tbsp Japanese soybean paste (miso paste)
1 tsp Chinese chili bean paste (doubanjiang)
Kosher salt, to taste

FOR THE SIMPLE CHASHU (OPTIONAL)

1 tbsp soy sauce
½ tbsp oyster sauce
1 tbsp mirin
½ tbsp granulated sugar
½ tbsp light corn syrup
¼ tsp dark soy sauce (optional)
1 tsp minced garlic
½ tsp freshly grated ginger
2 tbsp water
Small pinch of MSG (optional)
½ tbsp neutral-tasting oil
6 oz (180g) thinly sliced pork belly

1. To make the broth, in a large bowl, add the water, chicken bouillon powder, and Japanese bonito soup stock powder, and stir together until thoroughly combined. Set aside.
2. In a large wok or pot, heat 1½ tablespoons of lard over medium heat. Add the garlic, ginger, and white parts of the green onions, and sauté for 1 minute or until fragrant. Add the ground pork and white pepper. Break up the pork and sauté for 3 minutes or until the pork is cooked through.
3. Reduce the heat to low. Add the mirin, sugar, Japanese soybean paste, and Chinese chili bean paste, and stir together for 2 minutes. Add the stock and put it over a gentle heat. Taste and add salt to taste. (The broth does not have to be boiled.) Keep warm until ready to serve.
4. To make the simple chashu (if using), in a small bowl, stir together the soy sauce, oyster sauce, mirin, sugar, corn syrup, dark soy sauce (if using), garlic, ginger, water, and MSG (if using) until thoroughly combined.
5. In a large pan, add the oil and heat over medium heat. Once it gets nice and hot, add the pork belly. Cook for 3 minutes or until no longer pink. Pour the chashu sauce over the pork belly and gently simmer for another 3 minutes or until nicely glazed. Remove from the pan and set aside. Optionally, you can hit it with a blowtorch to get a nice char. (Prepare this simple chashu right before serving. If you make it ahead of time and let it sit for too long, the pork can become tough.)
6. In a medium pan, heat the remaining 1 tablespoon of lard (or neutral-tasting oil) over high heat. Once it gets nice and hot, add the mung bean sprouts and quickly stir-fry for 30 seconds to 1 minute. Remove from the pan and set aside.
7. To assemble, divide the ramen noodles and broth evenly between two serving bowls. Top with chashu (if using), soft-boiled eggs, mung bean sprouts, corn, green parts of the green onions, and dried seaweed (if using). Serve immediately.

TANTANMEN

Creamy and Spicy Sesame Ramen

PREP TIME: **15 minutes** // COOK TIME: **15 minutes** // SERVES: **2**

Here's another incredibly simple yet delicious ramen recipe. This popular Japanese ramen, tantanmen, is a variation of Sichuan's dan dan noodles. Originally designed to suit Japanese tastes, it has evolved into its own unique style. And now, this creamy, rich, and flavorful ramen has become one of the most beloved noodle soups around the world.

---

1 tbsp chili oil (or neutral-tasting oil), plus more to drizzle
7 oz (200g) ground pork
2 green onions, thinly sliced, white and green parts divided
2 garlic cloves, finely chopped
½ tsp freshly grated ginger
2 servings cooked ramen noodles
3½ oz (100g) mung bean sprouts (optional), blanched
2 baby bok choy (optional), halved or quartered lengthwise, blanched
Small pinch of toasted sesame seeds, to garnish
2 tbsp crushed roasted peanuts, to serve
1 soft-boiled egg, halved, to serve

FOR THE PORK TOPPING SAUCE

1 tbsp Chinese chili bean paste (doubanjiang)
1 tbsp oyster sauce
1 tbsp sake (or mirin, soju)
½ tsp granulated sugar

FOR THE SEASONING SAUCE (TARE)

2 tbsp Japanese sesame paste (neri goma) (or peanut butter)
1 tbsp chili oil
1 tsp white vinegar
2 tbsp soy sauce
1 tbsp mirin
¼ tsp Sichuan peppercorn oil (optional)

FOR THE BROTH

1 cup water
2 cups unsweetened soy milk
1 tbsp chicken bouillon powder

1. To make the pork topping sauce, in a small bowl, add all the sauce ingredients and stir together until thoroughly combined. Set aside.
2. In a large wok or pan, add the chili oil and heat over medium heat. Once it gets nice and hot, add the ground pork. Break up the pork and cook for 3 minutes or until it is no longer pink. Add the white parts of the green onions, garlic, and ginger, and sauté for 1 minute or until fragrant.
3. Increase the heat to high. Add in the pork topping sauce and stir-fry for 2 minutes or until the pork is cooked through and most of the liquid has evaporated. Turn off the heat. Set aside.
4. To make the seasoning sauce (tare), in a small bowl, whisk together all the ingredients until thoroughly combined. Set aside.
5. To make the broth, in a medium saucepan, whisk together the water, soy milk, and chicken bouillon powder until thoroughly combined. Place over low heat and gently simmer until it gets warm. (Do not cover the pot while simmering, as it can easily boil over.)
6. To assemble, add half of the seasoning sauce and half of the broth to each bowl. Stir to combine. Divide the ramen noodles evenly over the bowls and top with mung bean sprouts (if using), bok choy (if using), pork, green parts of the green onions, sesame seeds, peanuts, and soft-boiled egg. Drizzle with a little bit of chili oil. Serve immediately.

CLAIRE SAYS:

If you're doubting this ramen just because the broth isn't made with pork bone or chicken, you could be making one of the biggest mistakes of your life. Just one sip of this rich, creamy, and flavorful broth will transport you to a ramen restaurant somewhere in Japan. As Aaron always says, "This time, I guarantee it!"

CLAIRE SAYS:

I believe that this soupless tantanmen really stands out on hot summer days. When you're craving ramen but want to avoid sweating in the heat, try this creamy, flavor-packed, soupless dish. I'm sure everyone at the table will applaud your choice as the ideal dish for the occasion.

SHIRUNASHI TANTANMEN

Soupless Tantanmen

PREP TIME: **10 minutes** // COOK TIME: **10 minutes** // SERVES: **2**

By now, you've learned that tantanmen is a beautiful noodle soup born through a process of evolution. However, it has now taken another incredible step forward. These noodles—tossed in an aromatic, creamy, and slightly spicy peanut sauce without broth—have become simpler and more accessible, creating a massive sensation in the home-cooking ramen scene. Let's just embrace and enjoy the evolution of food!

---

2 tbsp neutral-tasting oil
2–3 green onions, thinly sliced, white and green parts divided
2 garlic cloves, finely chopped
½ tsp freshly grated ginger
7 oz (200g) ground pork
2 servings cooked ramen noodles
2 baby bok choy, halved or quartered lengthwise, blanched
2 soft-boiled eggs, halved, to serve
Japanese red pickled ginger (beni shoga) (optional), to serve

FOR THE PORK TOPPING SAUCE

1 tbsp Chinese chili bean paste (doubanjiang)
1 tbsp oyster sauce
1 tsp granulated sugar
1 tbsp mirin (or sake, soju)
Freshly cracked black pepper, to taste
¼ tsp Sichuan peppercorn oil (optional)

FOR THE TANTANMEN SAUCE (SEE NOTE)

2½ tbsp Japanese sesame paste (neri goma) (or tahini or peanut butter)
2 tbsp soy sauce
1 tbsp white vinegar
1 tsp granulated sugar
1 tbsp mirin
1 tbsp sake
1 tbsp chili oil
1 tbsp toasted sesame oil
½ tbsp chicken bouillon powder
½ tsp Sichuan peppercorn oil (optional)
Small pinch of Hondashi (Japanese bonito soup stock powder)
¼ cup hot water

1. To make the pork topping sauce, to a small bowl, add all the ingredients and stir together until thoroughly combined. Set aside.
2. In a large wok or pan, add the oil and heat over medium-high heat. Once it gets nice and hot, add the white parts of the green onions, garlic, and ginger, and sauté for 1 minute or until fragrant.
3. Add the ground pork. Break up the pork and cook for 3 minutes or until no longer pink. Add in the pork topping sauce and stir-fry for 2 to 3 minutes or until the pork is cooked through. Remove from the heat and set aside.
4. To make the tantanmen sauce, in a large bowl, whisk together all the ingredients until thoroughly combined (see note).
5. Add the cooked ramen noodles to the bowl and toss together until thoroughly coated.
6. Divide the noodles evenly between two serving bowls. Put a generous amount of pork topping on top. Garnish with bok choy, green onions, soft-boiled eggs, and pickled ginger (if using). Serve immediately.

NOTE: If you're cooking for kids or pregnant women, I recommend replacing mirin and sake with water. Since we don't boil this sauce, the alcohol will still remain in the sauce.

GROUND CHICKEN OYAKODON

Chicken and Egg Rice Bowl

PREP TIME: **8 minutes** // COOK TIME: **30 minutes** // SERVES: **4**

When I visited Tokyo, I discovered an oyakodon made with ground chicken, and it completely blew my mind. I felt like that's the ultimate version of a chicken rice bowl. So, I decided to recreate it in my own way. While this is not the most traditional version of oyakodon, I promise that just one bite will make you fall in love with it, just like I did in Tokyo. Do you want me to guarantee it? Sure! I guarantee it!

---

1 tbsp neutral-tasting oil
½ yellow onion, finely chopped
2 garlic cloves, finely chopped
½ tsp freshly grated ginger
17 oz (500g) boneless, skin-on chicken thighs, minced
8 large eggs, beaten, divided
Handful of Japanese parsley (mitsuba) (optional), roughly chopped, to garnish
4 cups hot cooked short-grain rice, about 7½ oz (210g) for each serving

FOR THE OYAKODON SAUCE

1 cup water
½ tbsp chicken bouillon powder
4½ tbsp soy sauce
4 tbsp mirin
½ tbsp granulated sugar
½ tsp Japanese bonito soup stock powder (Hondashi)

1. To make the oyakodon sauce, in a medium bowl, whisk together all the ingredients until thoroughly combined. (If you don't have Japanese bonito soup stock powder, you can replace it with chicken bouillon powder in this recipe.) Set aside.
2. In a large pot, add the oil and heat over medium-high heat. Once it gets nice and hot, add the onion, garlic, and ginger. Sauté for 2 to 3 minutes or until lightly browned.
3. Add the ground chicken. Cook, stirring occasionally, for 6 minutes or until most of the liquid has evaporated. Pour in the sauce, stir, and bring to a boil.
4. Once it comes to a boil, reduce the heat to medium-low. Cover and simmer, stirring occasionally, for 10 minutes. Set aside.
5. Make the oyakodon 1 portion at a time (see note). In a small pan, add ½ cup of meat sauce and bring to a boil over medium heat. Once it starts to boil, add in 2 beaten eggs. Top with some mitsuba (if using), cover, and cook for 1 to 2 minutes or until the eggs reach your desired doneness. (I recommend not overcooking the eggs because soft and runny eggs are the beauty of this dish.) Meanwhile, add one portion of rice to a serving bowl. Remove the oyakodon from the heat and slide over the rice. Repeat with the remaining ingredients and serve immediately.

NOTE: Oyakodon is usually cooked 1 portion at a time, using a specific pan called "oyakodon pan." However, if you don't have enough time or you're cooking for your family, you can use a larger pan, make 2 portions at a time, and divide them at the end.

CLAIRE SAYS:

This incredibly flavorful meat sauce is almost like a Japanese-style ragu. So, making a big batch and storing it in individual portions in the fridge or freezer can be a fantastic way to use it for meals over the next few days.

CLAIRE SAYS:

I must say this: adding a bit of mustard on top of kakuni is an absolute game-changer that completes this dish. So please, ignore Aaron's note that it's optional and trust me—try it together. You'll understand why I'm so insistent about this.

BUTA NO KAKUNI

Japanese Braised Pork Belly

PREP TIME: **15 minutes** // COOK TIME: **3 hours** // SERVES: **4–5**

When was the last time you had a bite of super tender meat that changed your life? What? You can't think of it? Don't worry about it. This succulent and melt-in-your-mouth pork belly, simmered in a sweet and savory Japanese sauce, will give you that unforgettable moment.

½ tbsp neutral-tasting oil
3.3 lb (1.5kg) skin-on pork belly, cut into 2-inch (5cm) cubes
1 small knob of ginger (about 15g), cut into thin slices
3 garlic cloves, smashed
1 yellow onion, cut in half
5–6 green onions
5 soft-boiled eggs (optional), halved, to serve
4 baby bok choy, halved or quartered lengthwise, blanched, to serve
Japanese mustard (karashi) (optional), to serve

FOR THE BRAISING LIQUID

4½ cups water
2 tsp Japanese bonito soup stock powder (Hondashi)
5½ tbsp soy sauce
5 tbsp mirin
½ cup sake
1 tbsp granulated sugar

1. To make the braising liquid, in a large bowl, whisk together all the ingredients until thoroughly combined. Set aside.
2. To a large pan, add the oil. Place the pork pieces skin-side down. Turn on the heat to medium-high. When the bottom turns golden brown, flip and sear all sides, about 12 minutes. (During this step, the oil might splatter, so using a splatter screen would be a great help.)
3. Once all sides of the pork belly are beautifully browned, transfer to a heavy-bottomed pot. (Place the pork pieces skin-side down.) Add the ginger, garlic, yellow onion, green onions, and braising liquid, and bring to a boil.
4. Once it comes to a boil, reduce the heat to low. Place a drop lid (otoshibuta) (see note) or a piece of parchment paper on top of the liquid. Simmer for 2½ hours.
5. Discard the ginger, garlic, yellow onion, and green onions. Carefully add your pork pieces onto a serving plate. Drizzle with the braising liquid. Garnish with soft-boiled eggs (if using), bok choy, and Japanese mustard (if using). Serve with hot rice.

NOTES: If you prefer a leaner and cleaner style for kakuni, pat the pork belly dry with a paper towel in Step 3 to remove any excess fat before transferring it.

The otoshibuta holds the ingredients steady in the liquid, preventing them from floating around and breaking apart while simmering.

KARAAGE

Japanese Fried Chicken

PREP TIME: **15 minutes + 30 minutes to marinate** // COOK TIME: **15 minutes** // SERVES: **4**

The week I first arrived in Sydney for university, I happened upon a tiny Japanese restaurant by chance. There, I found this bite-sized, lightly coated, juicy fried chicken. Ever since that day, it has held a permanent spot on my "World's Best Fried Chicken" list.

1.3 lb (600g) boneless skin-on chicken thighs or breasts, cut into 2-inch (5cm) pieces
1 cup potato starch (or cornstarch)
High-heat oil (such as canola, avocado, vegetable, etc.), for frying
4 cups shredded green cabbage, soaked in cold water and drained, to serve
Cherry tomatoes (optional), to serve
Lemon wedges (optional), to serve
Kewpie mayonnaise, to serve
Japanese seven spice (shichimi togarashi) (optional), to serve

FOR THE MARINADE

3 tbsp soy sauce
3 tbsp mirin
1 tsp granulated sugar
1 tsp minced garlic
1 tsp freshly grated ginger
½ cup water
½ tsp Japanese bonito soup stock powder (Hondashi)

FOR THE SESAME DRESSING (OPTIONAL)

3 tbsp toasted sesame seeds, ground
1 tbsp granulated sugar
5 tbsp Kewpie mayonnaise
1 tbsp white vinegar (or rice vinegar)
1 tsp soy sauce
½ tbsp toasted sesame oil
Kosher salt, to taste

1. To make the marinade, in a large bowl, whisk together all the ingredients until thoroughly combined.
2. Add the chicken in and gently toss together until thoroughly mixed. Cover and marinate in the fridge for at least 30 minutes or overnight.
3. Transfer the chicken to a strainer and drain well. Add the potato starch (or cornstarch) to a big tray. Grab some chicken pieces, lightly dredge them in the potato starch, and shake off the excess. Repeat with the remaining chicken pieces.
4. In a heavy-bottomed pot, heat about 2 inches (5cm) of cooking oil to 340°F (170°C). Working in batches, carefully place the chicken pieces in the oil (dropping them away from you). Fry for 2 to 3 minutes or until lightly browned. Remove from the hot oil and place on a wire rack to rest.
5. Add all the chicken pieces back into the pot and fry for 1 to 2 minutes until golden brown and cooked through. Transfer to the wire rack and rest.
6. To make the sesame dressing (if using), in a small bowl, whisk together all the dressing ingredients until thoroughly combined.
7. To serve, divide the karaage evenly between four serving plates. Add a generous amount of cabbage with: the sesame dressing (if using), cherry tomatoes (if using), and lemon wedges (if using). Garnish with Kewpie mayonnaise and top with Japanese seven spice (if using). Serve immediately.

CLAIRE SAYS:

Dipping karaage in Kewpie mayonnaise definitely makes it richer and more flavorful. However, if you're not a big fan of mayonnaise or if you are on a diet, try sprinkling a bit of salt instead. That small amount of salt will enhance the flavor in surprising ways.

CLAIRE SAYS:

The highlight of this shoyu ramen is definitely the fragrance from the aromatic oil. If you're thinking about skipping the step of making the aromatic oil and trying to make this ramen without it, I must insist—don't do it. It's absolutely essential.

SHOYU RAMEN

Soy Sauce–Based Ramen

PREP TIME: **10 minutes** // COOK TIME: **25 minutes** // SERVES: **2**

Compared to other types of ramen, shoyu ramen showcases the beauty of simplicity. In that sense, I have to admit that when I was younger, I didn't particularly like this simple noodle soup with its clear, soy sauce-based broth. However, as I've grown up, I have come to realize that the simple layers of flavor make it incredibly addictive. So now, if you were to ask me which ramen is my favorite, I would choose this shoyu ramen without hesitation.

---

4 cups water
1 tbsp chicken bouillon powder
1½ tsp Japanese bonito soup stock powder (Hondashi)
2 servings cooked ramen noodles
2 soft-boiled eggs, halved, to serve
1 Japanese fish cake (narutomaki) (optional), thinly sliced, to serve
Dried seaweed (optional), to serve

FOR THE AROMATIC OIL

5 tbsp lard (or neutral-tasting oil)
2–3 green onions, thinly sliced, plus more to garnish
1 small knob of ginger (12g), finely chopped

FOR THE SEASONING SAUCE (TARE)

4 tbsp soy sauce
½ tsp granulated sugar
1 tsp mirin
Small pinch of MSG (optional)

FOR THE SIMPLE CHASHU

1 tbsp soy sauce
½ tbsp oyster sauce
1 tbsp mirin
½ tbsp granulated sugar
½ tbsp light corn syrup
¼ tsp dark soy sauce (optional)
1 tsp minced garlic
½ tsp freshly grated ginger
2 tbsp water
Small pinch of MSG (optional)
½ tbsp neutral-tasting oil
6 oz (180g) thinly sliced pork belly

1. To make the aromatic oil, in a small saucepan, heat the lard (or oil) over medium-low heat. Once the lard is melted, add the green onions and ginger and sauté for 3 to 4 minutes or until fragrant. Remove from the heat and strain out the green onions and ginger. Set aside.
2. To make the seasoning sauce (tare), in a small bowl, whisk together all the ingredients until thoroughly combined. Set aside.
3. In a medium pot, add the water, chicken bouillon powder, and Japanese bonito soup stock powder, and put it on a gentle heat. Keep warm until ready to serve.
4. To make the simple chashu, in a small bowl, stir together the soy sauce, oyster sauce, mirin, sugar, corn syrup, dark soy sauce (if using), garlic, ginger, water, and MSG (if using) until thoroughly combined.
5. To a large pan, add the oil and heat over medium heat. Once it gets nice and hot, add the pork belly and cook for 3 minutes or until no longer pink. Pour the chashu sauce over the pork belly and gently simmer for another 3 minutes or until nicely glazed. Remove from the pan and set aside. Optionally, you can hit it with a blowtorch to get a nice char. (Prepare this simple chashu right before serving. If you make it ahead of time and let it sit for too long, the pork can become tough.)
6. To serve, in each serving bowl, whisk together 1 tablespoon of seasoning sauce (tare), 1 tablespoon of aromatic oil, and half of the broth until thoroughly combined. Taste and add more seasoning sauce if needed. Add the ramen noodles. Top with chashu, green onions, soft-boiled eggs, fish cake (if using), and dried seaweed (if using). Serve immediately.

NIKU UDON

Beef Udon Noodle Soup

PREP TIME: **10 minutes** // COOK TIME: **15 minutes** // SERVES: **2**

Many people tell Claire how lucky she is to enjoy a wide variety of delicious dishes every day. However, the truth is far from that. Like many of you, I'm busy with various tasks during the week. That's why I often whip up quick and easy dinners in under 15 minutes. This routine inspired the series "This 15-Minute Something Will Change Your Life." And among all the recipes, this comforting and heartwarming Japanese beef noodle soup is one of our absolute favorites during soup season.

---

1 tbsp neutral-tasting oil
11 oz (300g) thinly sliced beef (ribeye, tenderloin, etc.), cut into bite-sized pieces
½ yellow onion, thinly sliced
2 servings udon noodles
1 Japanese fish cake (narutomaki) (optional), thinly sliced, to serve
1 soft-boiled egg, halved, to serve
1–2 green onions, thinly sliced, to serve

FOR THE DASHI BROTH

4 cups water
2 tbsp soy sauce
2 tbsp mirin
1½ tsp Japanese bonito soup stock powder (Hondashi)

FOR THE BEEF TOPPING SAUCE

2 tbsp soy sauce
1 tbsp granulated sugar
1½ tbsp mirin
½ tsp freshly grated ginger

1. To prepare the dashi broth, in a large pot, whisk together all the ingredients and bring to a boil. Once it starts boiling and bubbling, turn off the heat. Taste and add more salt if needed. Cover and keep warm.
2. To make the beef topping sauce, in a small bowl, whisk together all the ingredients until thoroughly combined. Set aside.
3. In a medium pan, heat the oil over medium-high heat. Once it gets nice and hot, add the beef and onion and stir-fry for 2 minutes or until the beef is no longer pink. Add the beef topping sauce and cook for 2 to 3 minutes or until the beef is cooked through. Turn off the heat and set aside.
4. Meanwhile, bring a pot of water to a boil. Cook the noodles according to the package instructions. Ladle some noodle cooking water out into your serving bowls. Once the bowls are heated, dump the water out.
5. To serve, divide the drained noodles between the serving bowls. Gently add some broth over the noodles. Top with the beef, fish cake (if using), soft-boiled egg, and green onions. Serve immediately.

NOTE: If you can't get thinly sliced beef, place a chunk of meat in a resealable plastic bag and freeze it for about 30 minutes. Once it's firm but not fully frozen, slice it thinly against the grain.

CLAIRE SAYS:

A great tip for enhancing the flavor of udon broth is to generously pile on the green onions. Yes, this is yet another moment where Aaron's famous saying applies. So remember: More green onion, more delicious!

CLAIRE SAYS:

The most beautiful part of this dish is the broth. It is infused with the natural sweetness of the vegetables, the deep umami of the dashi, and the richness of the beef. Each ingredient adds to its layers of complexity. Take your time to savor the broth; it promises to be an incredibly enjoyable experience.

KARE UDON

Japanese Curry Udon Noodle Soup

PREP TIME: **15 minutes** // COOK TIME: **15 minutes** // SERVES: **3**

Are you a fan of Japanese curry? How about chewy udon noodles? I doubt you could say no to either. They are all great, right? That's exactly why the Japanese brought them together to create this slightly spicy, richly flavorful, curry udon noodle soup. It became a lunchtime favorite all across Japan, and now, it's about to become your favorite too.

½ carrot (90g), roughly chopped
½ yellow onion, roughly chopped
2 garlic cloves
1 small knob of ginger (about 4g), peeled
2 tbsp neutral-tasting oil
11 oz (300g) thinly sliced beef or chicken thigh, cut into bite-sized pieces
2 tbsp unsalted butter
1 tsp tomato paste
1 tbsp curry powder (preferably Japanese)
1 tbsp all-purpose flour
Small pinch of MSG (optional)
3 servings udon noodles
3 soft-boiled eggs (optional), halved, to serve
1–2 green onions, thinly sliced

FOR THE DASHI BROTH

4 cups water
1 tbsp soy sauce
2 tbsp mirin
1 tbsp chicken bouillon powder
1 tsp Worcestershire sauce (optional)
1 tsp Japanese bonito soup stock powder (Hondashi)

1. To a blender, add the carrot, onion, garlic, and ginger. Blend on high speed until completely smooth. Set aside.
2. In a large pan, heat the oil over high heat. Once it's heated, add the beef and cook for 2 to 3 minutes or until it is nicely browned and cooked through. Remove from the pan and set aside.
3. To the same pan over medium-high heat, add the vegetable puree and cook for 2 to 3 minutes or until most of the liquid has evaporated. Make sure to keep stirring it.
4. Reduce the heat to low. Add the butter, tomato paste, curry powder, and all-purpose flour. Give a good stir for 1 to 2 minutes or until thoroughly combined. Remove from the heat and set aside.
5. To make the dashi broth, in a large pot, whisk together all the ingredients until thoroughly combined. Bring to a boil. Once it comes to a boil, add the cooked beef, curry paste, and MSG (if using), and simmer for 3 minutes. Give a good stir until there are no lumps in it.
6. Meanwhile, bring a pot of water to a boil. Cook the noodles according to the package instructions and drain well.
7. To serve, divide the drained noodles evenly between three serving bowls. Gently add some broth and beef over the noodles. Top with soft-boiled eggs (if using) and green onions. Serve immediately.

SHOGAYAKI

Ginger Pork

PREP TIME: **10 minutes** // COOK TIME: **15 minutes** // SERVES: **2**

There's something I always say on my YouTube channel and blog: "Pork and ginger are a match made in heaven." I believe this Japanese ginger pork recipe is evidence number one. Thinly sliced pork simmered in a rich, flavorful ginger sauce will undoubtedly prove to you what the ultimate pairing truly is.

---

13 oz (360g) pork loin (or pork shoulder), thinly sliced

Freshly cracked black pepper, to taste

Kosher salt, to taste

2 tbsp potato starch (or cornstarch, all-purpose flour)

3 tbsp neutral-tasting oil, divided

½ yellow onion, thinly sliced

Handful of shishito peppers (optional), to garnish

2 cups shredded green cabbage (see note), to serve

Cherry tomatoes (optional), to serve

FOR THE GINGER SAUCE

1 tbsp freshly grated ginger

3 tbsp soy sauce

3 tbsp mirin

3 tbsp sake

2 tsp granulated sugar

1 tbsp water

1. To make the ginger sauce, in a small bowl, whisk together all the ingredients until thoroughly combined. Set aside.
2. Make a few slashes along the edges of each pork slice to prevent curling while cooking. Season both sides with black pepper. If the slices are thicker than ⅛ inch (3mm), lightly season with salt. Lightly coat the pork pieces with potato starch.
3. In a large pan, heat 1 tablespoon of oil over medium-high heat. Add the onion with a pinch of salt. Sauté for 3 to 4 minutes or until softened and browned. Remove from the pan and set aside.
4. In the same pan, add 1 tablespoon of oil over medium-high heat. Once it gets nice and hot, working in two batches, add the pork slices in a single layer. Cook for 1 to 2 minutes on each side or until no longer pink. Do not overcook, as pork can easily become dry and tough.
5. Once both batches are done, reduce the heat to medium. Add all the pork pieces and onion back into the pan. Give the ginger sauce a quick stir and pour in. Simmer for 2 to 3 minutes, or until the sauce thickens, flipping the pork pieces occasionally to coat well.
6. Meanwhile, grill some shishito peppers (if using) to use as a garnish.
7. To serve, place half of the shredded cabbage and the ginger pork on each plate. Drizzle some sauce from the pan over the pork. Add grilled shishito peppers and cherry tomatoes (if using) on the side. Serve with hot rice.

NOTE: Soak the shredded cabbage in cold water for 2 minutes. This will remove any bitterness and keep it crisp and fresh.

CLAIRE SAYS:

Serving raw cabbage without any dressing may seem strange at first. However, when paired with the richly flavored ginger sauce or the onions that picked up the sauce, you'll totally understand why it's served this way. So, don't skip the cabbage—be sure to include it alongside your dish. It's all part of Aaron's thoughtfully designed intention.

CLAIRE SAYS:

Chicken nanban is not the ultra-crispy fried chicken you might expect from Korean fried chicken. Instead, it's coated in a soft egg batter that absorbs a savory, sweet, and tangy sauce, enhancing the flavor of the juicy, tender chicken inside. For this reason, I highly recommend enjoying it with hot rice rather than on its own; the combination of the chicken and rice is truly exceptional.

CHICKEN NANBAN

Japanese Fried Chicken with Tartar Sauce

PREP TIME: **20 minutes** // COOK TIME: **15 minutes** // SERVES: **2**

Whenever I visit Japan, especially Kyushu (the southernmost of the main islands of Japan), I always make sure to have this dish because the combination of juicy fried chicken and creamy tartar sauce never disappoints. Yes, with every single bite, I am reminded that this is truly one of the best fried chicken dishes around the world.

---

1 lb (450g) boneless skin-on chicken thighs (or breasts)
Kosher salt, to taste
Freshly cracked black pepper, to taste
¼ cup all-purpose flour
1–2 large eggs
High-heat oil (such as canola, avocado, vegetable, etc.), for frying
Lettuce and shredded green cabbage (or salad greens), to serve
Cherry tomatoes, to serve

FOR THE NANBAN SAUCE

2 tbsp soy sauce
2 tbsp white vinegar (or rice vinegar)
2 tbsp granulated sugar
1 tbsp mirin

FOR THE TARTAR SAUCE

2 hard-boiled eggs, finely chopped
¼ yellow onion, finely chopped, soaked in cold water for 10 minutes and drained well
1 green onion, thinly sliced
4 tbsp Kewpie mayonnaise
1 tsp lemon juice
½ tbsp ketchup
Kosher salt and freshly cracked black pepper, to taste

1. To make the nanban sauce, in a small saucepan, whisk together all the ingredients until thoroughly combined. Bring to a rapid boil over high heat. Cook, stirring frequently, for 2 minutes or until the sugar is completely dissolved. Remove from the heat and set aside.
2. To make the tartar sauce, in a medium bowl, add all the ingredients and mix until everything is thoroughly combined. Taste and add more salt and pepper if needed. Set aside.
3. Trim off any excess fat or skin from the chicken, if desired. To ensure even cooking, gently pound the chicken with the back of a knife until even in thickness. Make small cuts along the edges to prevent curling while frying. Lightly season both sides with salt and pepper. Set aside.
4. Prepare two separate bowls or trays for the breading station. To the first, add the all-purpose flour. In the second, beat the eggs until well mixed.
5. Evenly coat each piece of chicken in the flour and shake off any excess. Thoroughly coat the chicken in the egg wash. Make sure there are no dry spots.
6. In a large Dutch oven or heavy-bottomed pot, heat about 2 inches (5cm) of cooking oil to 340°F (170°C). Working in batches, carefully place the chicken in the oil, skin-side down. Fry for 7 to 8 minutes or until golden brown and cooked through. Remove from the hot oil and let rest on a wire rack. Repeat with the remaining chicken pieces. When all the chicken is cooked, coat the chicken in the nanban sauce.
7. To serve, arrange some lettuce and shredded cabbage on a plate. Place the fried chicken on the side and top with a generous amount of tartar sauce. Garnish with cherry tomatoes and serve with hot rice.

OMURICE

Omelet Rice

PREP TIME: **10 minutes** // COOK TIME: **20 minutes** // SERVES: **2**

When I began writing this book, I promised myself that I wouldn't start with the lame cliché: "When I was a child..." However, for this nostalgic dish, I had to make an exception. The flavorful fried rice, soft omelet, and creamy, buttery sauce have been the perfect meal from my childhood till now. (Although the dish originated in Japan, omurice is also very popular in Korea.)

---

3 tbsp neutral-tasting oil, divided
4.2 oz (120g) ground beef (or pork, chicken, etc.)
1 garlic clove, finely chopped
¼ carrot (45g), finely chopped
¼ yellow onion, finely chopped
2 cups cooked and cooled short-grain rice, preferably day-old rice
Kosher salt and freshly cracked black pepper, to taste
6 large eggs
Heavy cream or sour cream (optional), to drizzle
Finely chopped parsley (optional), to garnish

FOR THE OMURICE SAUCE

2 tbsp unsalted butter
2 tbsp all-purpose flour
1 cup water
½ tbsp granulated sugar
1 tbsp mirin
2 tbsp ketchup
2 tbsp Worcestershire sauce
½ tbsp chicken bouillon powder
Freshly cracked black pepper, to taste

FOR THE FRIED RICE SAUCE

2 tbsp ketchup
2 tbsp mirin
2 tbsp Worcestershire sauce

1. To make the omurice sauce, to a small saucepan, add the butter and place over low heat. Once the butter is melted, add the flour and stir well for 4 to 5 minutes. Once it turns brown, add the water little by little and stir until thoroughly combined.
2. Add the sugar, mirin, ketchup, Worcestershire sauce, chicken bouillon powder, and black pepper, and give it a good stir. Bring to a boil and simmer for 3 more minutes. Remove from the heat and set aside. Keep warm.
3. To make the fried rice sauce, in a small bowl, mix all the ingredients until thoroughly combined. Set aside.
4. In a large pan, heat 1 tablespoon of oil over medium-high heat. Once it gets nice and hot, add the ground beef. Break up the beef and cook for 2 to 3 minutes or until it begins to brown. Add the garlic, carrot, onion, and fried rice sauce, and stir-fry for 2 to 3 minutes or until the onion becomes translucent.
5. Increase the heat to high and add the rice. Using a spatula, break the rice up and stir-fry for 3 to 4 minutes or until every single grain is coated well. Taste and add more salt and pepper to taste. Divide the fried rice between two small bowls and gently press down. Cover with serving plates and flip. Keep warm and set aside.
6. In a large mixing bowl, beat the eggs with a pinch of salt. In a medium pan, heat 1 tablespoon of oil over medium heat. Once it's nice and hot, add half of the beaten eggs and cook for 1 minute or until the bottom is cooked but the top is still a bit runny. Gently cover one portion of fried rice with the omelet. Repeat with the remaining eggs.
7. To serve, pour half of the omurice sauce over each omelet. Garnish with heavy cream and parsley, if using. Serve immediately.

CLAIRE SAYS:

When I was a little kid, I hated carrots! But my mom's omurice was packed with them. Even though I was a carrot hater, I could not say no to her omurice because it was my absolute favorite dish. So, if you have a picky eater at home, serve them this dish. I'm sure the same magic will happen for them as it did for me.

CLAIRE SAYS:

If you want to dramatically reduce the cooking time further, using teriyaki sauce (page 136) instead of making a separate butadon sauce is a great option. Pretty good tip, right?

BUTADON

Pork Rice Bowl

PREP TIME: **5 minutes** // COOK TIME: **15 minutes** // SERVES: **2**

Have you ever had one of those days when you want a quick and simple dinner, but also something that feels a bit fancy? On those days, I always make this Japanese pork rice bowl. A warm bowl of steamed rice topped with perfectly caramelized pork in a sweet and savory sauce—this pork rice bowl not only satisfies your taste buds, but it's also a dish that's stylish. It's time to take a picture and show it off on your social media!

---

2 garlic cloves, smashed
1 small knob of ginger (about 6g), cut into thin slices
1 tsp neutral-tasting oil
1.3 lb (600g) thinly sliced (about ¼-inch (0.5cm) thick) pork belly
2 cups hot cooked short-grain rice, about 7½ oz (210g) for each serving
1 soft-boiled egg (optional), halved, to serve
1–2 green onions, thinly sliced, to garnish

FOR THE BUTADON SAUCE

½ cup soy sauce
½ cup sake
½ cup mirin
2 tbsp granulated sugar
½ tsp Japanese bonito soup stock powder (Hondashi)

1. To make the butadon sauce, in a medium saucepan, whisk together all the ingredients until thoroughly combined. Add the garlic and ginger and bring to a boil. Reduce the heat to medium and simmer for 5 minutes. Turn off the heat and discard the solids. Set aside. (Once cooled, you can put it in an airtight container and keep it in the fridge for up to 1 month.)
2. To a large pan, add the oil. Use paper towels to coat the bottom of the pan with the oil and preheat over medium-high heat. Once heated, add the pork belly and sear for 1 minute or until lightly browned. Flip and sear the other side for another 1 to 2 minutes or until lightly browned. Do not overcook it. The pork will be cooked more with the butadon sauce later.
3. Reduce the heat to low. Generously brush the pork pieces with butadon sauce. (You could just pour some sauce over them instead of brushing.) Keep moving and flipping the pork pieces and coat with the sauce in the pan.
4. When the pork is cooked through and coated with the sauce, remove from the pan and cut into 2-inch (5cm) or bite-sized pieces.
5. To serve, divide the rice evenly between two serving bowls. Drizzle 1 teaspoon of butadon sauce over the rice. Arrange the pork pieces in a flower pattern. Optionally, use a blowtorch to brown the glaze until lightly charred. Garnish with soft-boiled egg (if using) and green onions. Serve immediately.

NOTE: If you don't serve immediately and it sits for too long, the pork can become tough.

SOBORO DON

Ground Chicken Rice Bowl

PREP TIME: **5 minutes** // COOK TIME: **10 minutes** // SERVES: **2**

Sometimes, life throws you a challenge: preparing a meal that satisfies both kids and adults alike. On those occasions, this simple and comforting Japanese rice bowl will have you covered. With savory and flavorful ground chicken, fluffy scrambled eggs, and fresh green onions all in one bowl, it's a dish sure to bring happiness and harmony to your dinner table.

---

7 oz (200g) ground chicken (or beef, pork, tofu, etc.)
2 green onions, thinly sliced, white and green parts divided
2 garlic cloves, finely chopped
½ tsp freshly grated ginger
4 large eggs
Kosher salt and freshly cracked black pepper, to taste
2 tbsp unsalted butter
1 tbsp neutral-tasting oil
2 cups hot cooked short-grain rice, about 7½ oz (210g) for each serving
2 fresh egg yolks (optional), to serve (see note)

FOR THE MARINADE

1½ tbsp soy sauce
½ tbsp granulated sugar
1 tbsp mirin
1 tbsp sake (or soju, dry sherry, water, etc.)
1 tbsp oyster sauce
Freshly cracked black pepper, to taste

1. To marinate the chicken, in a large bowl, combine the ground chicken and all the marinade ingredients until thoroughly mixed. Add the white parts of the green onions, garlic, and ginger, and mix well. Cover with plastic wrap and set aside.
2. In a medium bowl, beat the eggs with salt and pepper. Place a large pan over medium heat. Add the butter. Once the butter is melted, add the beaten eggs and scramble for 2 minutes or until it reaches your desired doneness. Remove from the pan and set aside.
3. In the same pan, add the oil over high heat. Once it's heated, add the marinated chicken and cook for 4 to 5 minutes. Make sure to evaporate most of the liquid and keep tossing around until it gets crumbly. When the chicken is cooked through and nicely browned, turn off the heat.
4. To serve, divide the rice evenly between two serving bowls. Top with the chicken on one side of the bowls and the scrambled eggs on the other. Add a generous amount of green onions between the chicken and eggs. Top with the fresh egg yolks (if using). Serve immediately and enjoy.

NOTE: I used a raw egg yolk as a garnish, but if you are not sure about the freshness of the eggs, feel free to skip them or substitute with poached eggs or sunny-side up eggs instead.

CLAIRE SAYS:

This soboro don isn't just a great weeknight dinner option that appeals to all generations. It's also a beloved choice for packed lunches.

CLAIRE SAYS:

Japanese red pickled ginger (beni shoga) isn't essential for this dish, but it adds a significant flavor boost—similar to how kimchi enhances Korean dishes. Its gingery flavor and tanginess boost up the flavor of yakisoba. So I recommend keeping some in your fridge, just like we do. It's perfect for pairing with other Japanese dishes as well!

YAKISOBA

Japanese Stir-Fried Noodles

PREP TIME: **10 minutes** // COOK TIME: **15 minutes** // SERVES: **2**

Here comes the king of Japanese street food, yakisoba. Once you slurp these Japanese stir-fried noodles with meat and vegetables in a sweet, savory, and slightly tangy sauce, trust me, you will find yourself making this dish over and over again. I guarantee it!

---

1 tbsp neutral-tasting oil, divided
7 oz (200g) thinly sliced pork belly (or chicken, shrimp, firm tofu), cut into bite-sized pieces
2 green onions, the tops cut into 2-inch (5cm) pieces, plus thinly sliced white parts
2 garlic cloves, finely chopped
1 tsp freshly grated ginger
3½ oz (100g) green cabbage leaves, cut into bite-sized pieces
½ yellow onion, thinly sliced
⅓ carrot (60g), cut into thin matchsticks
3 white button mushrooms, thinly sliced
Kosher salt and freshly cracked black pepper, to taste
2 servings cooked yakisoba noodles (or spaghetti, udon noodles, etc.)
Dried bonito flakes (katsuobushi) (optional), to serve
Dried green seaweed (aonori) (optional), to serve
Japanese red pickled ginger (beni shoga) (optional), to serve

FOR THE SAUCE

2 tbsp soy sauce
1 tbsp oyster sauce
1 tbsp ketchup
1 tbsp granulated sugar
1 tbsp Worcestershire sauce
1 tbsp mirin

1. To make the sauce, in a small bowl, whisk together all the ingredients until thoroughly combined. Set aside.
2. To a large wok or pan, add ½ tablespoon of oil and heat over medium-high heat. Once it gets nice and hot, add the pork belly in a single layer. Cook for 2 minutes or until no longer pink.
3. Add the white parts of the green onions, garlic, and ginger, and sauté for 1 minute or until fragrant. Add the cabbage, onion, carrot, mushrooms, and the green parts of the green onions. Season with salt and pepper. Stir-fry for 3 minutes or until the vegetables are softened. Remove from the wok and set aside.
4. In the same wok, add the remaining ½ tablespoon of oil and heat over medium-high heat. Add the noodles and spread them out. Let sit for 2 minutes or until the noodles are browned and crisp up a little bit. Flip and gently separate the noodles using tongs or chopsticks.
5. Add half of the sauce and toss together for 1 minute or until the noodles are beautifully coated. Add the pork and vegetables back into the wok, along with the remaining sauce. Toss everything together for 2 minutes or until everything is nicely coated.
6. To serve, divide the noodles evenly between two serving bowls. Top with some bonito flakes, dried green seaweed, and pickled ginger, if using. Serve immediately.

MAZESOBA

Brothless Ramen

PREP TIME: **15 minutes** // COOK TIME: **10 minutes** // SERVES: **2**

In this book, I've shared a variety of ramen recipes that are incredibly easy to make. But if you still haven't tried any, this is my last invitation card. Mazesoba, also known as Taiwan mazeaoba, is a creamy and aromatic specialty from Nagoya that will take you to a tasty wonderland you'll never want to leave.

---

2 tbsp neutral-tasting oil
2 green onions, thinly sliced, white and green parts divided
4 garlic cloves, finely chopped, divided
½ tsp freshly grated ginger
7 oz (200g) ground pork
2 servings cooked mazesoba noodles (or thick ramen noodles)
1 tbsp toasted sesame oil
½ tbsp chili oil (optional)
1 tsp chicken bouillon powder
Freshly cracked black pepper, to taste
1½ oz (40g) garlic chives, cut into ⅛-inch (0.3cm) pieces
1 sheet dried seaweed, cut into 1-inch (2.5cm) thin strips
½ cup dried bonito flakes, finely ground (see note)
4 tbsp tempura scraps (tenkasu)
2 egg yolks (optional) (see note)

FOR THE PORK TOPPING SAUCE

1 tbsp Chinese chili bean paste (doubanjiang)
1 tbsp oyster sauce
1 tsp granulated sugar
1 tbsp mirin
Freshly cracked black pepper

1. To make the pork topping sauce, in a small bowl, whisk together all the ingredients until thoroughly combined. Set aside.
2. In a wok or medium pan, heat the oil over medium-high heat. Once it's heated, add the white parts of the green onions, half of the garlic, and the ginger, and sauté for 1 minute or until fragrant.
3. Add the ground pork. Break into little pieces and cook for 3 minutes or until no longer pink. Add the pork topping sauce and stir-fry for 2 minutes or until the pork is cooked through. Remove from the heat and set aside.
4. To a large bowl, add the cooked noodles, sesame oil, chili oil (if using), chicken bouillon powder, and black pepper to taste. Toss together until the noodles are nicely coated. (Add a few tablespoons of the noodle cooking water if needed.)
5. To serve, divide the noodles evenly between two serving bowls. Nicely arrange the garlic chives, the remaining chopped garlic, dried seaweed, green parts of green onions, ground bonito flakes, and tempura scraps on top of the noodles. Place the pork topping in the center and top with an egg yolk (if using). Serve immediately.

NOTES: If you microwave the bonito flakes for 1 minute before grinding, they will be much easier to grind.

I used raw egg yolks as a garnish and as a part of the sauce, but if you are not sure about the freshness of the eggs, feel free to skip them or substitute with poached eggs or sunny-side up eggs instead.

CLAIRE SAYS:

Here's a pro tip for enjoying mazesoba: when you're about halfway through, add about ½ tablespoon of vinegar. It'll feel like you're enjoying two different versions of mazesoba in one meal!

CLAIRE SAYS:

If you prefer a creamier style, feel free to add a bit more Kewpie mayo. I personally like to add a little extra. For an extra flavor boost, you can also try spreading some salted butter on the bread. You're welcome!

TAMAGO SANDO

Japanese Egg Sandwich

PREP TIME: **5 minutes** // COOK TIME: **15 minutes** // MAKES: **4**

Sure, I could use all kinds of fancy words to describe this Japanese egg sandwich, but some people might think, *An egg sandwich is just an egg sandwich*. Let me tell you, though—you could not be more wrong. Every year, millions of tourists visiting Japan stop at the convenience store to grab this sandwich for its ultra-creamy egg filling and soft, pillowy white bread.

---

8 large eggs
Generous pinch of kosher salt, to taste
Freshly cracked black pepper, to taste
5 tbsp Kewpie mayonnaise
1 tbsp heavy cream (or whole milk)
8 thick slices white bread (or brioche)

1. Bring a pot of water to a boil. Once it starts to boil, carefully lower the eggs in. Boil for 12 minutes. Shock them in ice water. Peel the eggs and separate the yolks and whites.
2. In a medium bowl, press the yolks through a fine sieve. Then do the same thing with the egg whites. (If you want a chunky texture, you can cut the whites into small pieces with a knife instead.)
3. To the eggs, add a generous pinch of salt, black pepper, Kewpie mayonnaise, and heavy cream. Mix well until thoroughly combined.
4. To serve, spread a generous amount of egg filling on a slice of the bread. Cover with another slice of the bread. Repeat with the remaining egg filling and bread. Optionally, cut the crusts off the bread. Enjoy!

KOROKKE

Japanese Potato Croquettes

PREP TIME: **15 minutes** // COOK TIME: **40 minutes** // MAKES: **5**

Warning: These Japanese-style croquettes, filled with creamy mashed potatoes infused with an umami sauce and coated in panko for a crispy, katsu-like finish, might cause a serious addiction.

---

3 Yukon Gold potatoes (about 300g), peeled and diced
1 tbsp neutral-tasting oil
2 oz (50g) ground beef
¼ carrot, finely chopped
¼ yellow onion, finely chopped
1 tbsp unsalted butter, melted
Freshly cracked black pepper, to taste
½ cup all-purpose flour
2 large eggs
2 cups panko breadcrumbs
High-heat oil (such as canola, avocado, vegetable, etc.), for frying
Salad greens, to serve
Ketchup, to serve

FOR THE SAUCE

1 tbsp soy sauce
1 tbsp oyster sauce
6 tbsp mirin

1. Bring a pot of water to a boil, then reduce the heat to low. Add the potatoes and cook for 25 minutes or until cooked through. Drain the potatoes and mash. Set aside.
2. To make the sauce, in a medium bowl, whisk together all the ingredients until thoroughly combined. Set aside.
3. In a medium pan, heat the oil over medium-high heat. Once it gets nice and hot, add the ground beef. Break up the beef so that it doesn't clump together. Cook for 1 minute or until no longer pink. Add the carrot and onion and stir-fry for 3 to 4 minutes or until the onion starts to brown.
4. Add the sauce and bring to a boil over high heat. Once it starts boiling and bubbling, simmer for 1 minute. Strain out the sauce with a fine sieve and set aside. Do not throw the sauce away.
5. To the mashed potatoes, add the strained beef and vegetables, butter, and black pepper. Mix the potato mixture until thoroughly combined. Taste and add 1 or 2 teaspoons of the sauce, if needed.
6. Portion the potato mixture into 5 even balls and form into patties. Place on a plate or tray. Cover and let cool to room temperature.
7. Prepare three separate bowls or trays for the breading station. To the first, add the all-purpose flour. In the second, beat the eggs until well mixed. And to the third, add the panko breadcrumbs.
8. Evenly coat a patty in the flour and shake off any excess. Next, thoroughly coat the patty in the egg wash. Make sure there are no dry spots. Lastly, cover with a good amount of breadcrumbs and press down so that they can stick to the surface. Repeat with the remaining patties.
9. In a large Dutch oven or heavy-bottomed pot, heat about 2 inches (5cm) of cooking oil to 340°F (170°C). Carefully place the patties in the oil. Fry for 4 to 5 minutes or until crispy golden brown. Remove from the hot oil and drain on a wire rack. Serve immediately with salad greens, ketchup, and katsu sauce (page 139).

NOTE: Since the inside of the croquette is already cooked, simply deep-fry until golden brown. Alternatively, you can spray some oil on the surface of the patties and cook them in an air fryer.

CLAIRE SAYS:

If you're a big fan of cheese, try adding some mozzarella cheese when shaping the croquette patties. With the crispy exterior, creamy interior, and beautiful cheese pull, it will become even more addictive!

CLAIRE SAYS:

This recipe features a simple pan-frying method so that everyone can easily enjoy it. However, if you're looking for a juicier, upgraded version of the steak rice bowl, be sure to visit our YouTube channel or blog. There, you'll find a recipe that features reverse-seared steak.

STEAK DONBURI

Steak Rice Bowl

PREP TIME: **5 minutes** // COOK TIME: **12 minutes** // SERVES: **2**

Perfectly cooked steak, freshly cooked rice, and a special Japanese-style sauce that is packed with umami—this is the rice bowl that every person on the planet has dreamed of.

---

1 lb (450g) New York strip steak, about 1¼ to 1½ inches (3–3.8cm) thick
Kosher salt and freshly cracked black pepper, to taste
2-3 tbsp neutral-tasting oil
½ yellow onion, thinly sliced
2 cups hot cooked short-grain rice, about 7½ oz (210g) for each serving
2 raw egg yolks (optional), to serve (see note)
1 green onion, thinly sliced, to garnish
Microgreens (or salad greens), to serve
Fresh wasabi, to serve

FOR THE SAUCE

5 tbsp soy sauce
½ tbsp oyster sauce
1½ tbsp granulated sugar
3 tbsp mirin
2 tbsp sake

1. To make the sauce, in a small bowl, whisk together all the ingredients until thoroughly combined. Set aside.
2. Pat the steak completely dry on all sides. Season with salt and pepper. (You don't have to season it too generously because we have a sauce for the steak.)
3. In a medium pan or skillet, heat the oil over medium-high heat. Once it gets extremely hot and nearly smoking, carefully add the steak and sear for 2 to 3 minutes or until it gets a deep brown crust on the bottom. Flip and sear for an additional 3 minutes. At this point, your steak should be nearing medium rare. If your cut is thicker than 1½ inches (3.8cm), let it cook a bit longer.
4. Sear the fat side for 1 minute or until golden brown. Keep moving the steak and sear every side for 30 seconds or until the steak reaches medium-rare and an internal temperature of 132°F (56°C). Remove from the pan and let rest, uncovered, for 5 minutes.
5. Meanwhile, in the same pan over medium-low heat, add the onion and sauté for 1 minute or until fragrant. Add the sauce and let simmer for 3 minutes or until it thickens slightly. Separate the onion and the sauce with a fine sieve. Set aside.
6. Thinly slice the steak so that it's easy to bite into. (You can go thicker or even cube the steak if you prefer.)
7. To serve, add 1 cup of cooked rice to each serving bowl. Layer the onion on top, followed by the steak slices. Drizzle a bit of sauce over the top. Gently place an egg yolk (if using) on top of the steak. Garnish with green onion, microgreens, and a dab of wasabi for an extra kick. Serve immediately.

NOTE: I used raw egg yolks as a garnish and as a part of the sauce, but if you are not sure about the freshness of the eggs, feel free to skip them or substitute with poached eggs or sunny-side up eggs instead.

CHINESE

MAPO TOFU

Spicy Sichuan Tofu with Ground Pork

PREP TIME: **10 minutes** // COOK TIME: **15 minutes** // SERVES: **2–3**

Through countless recipes, I've worked hard to prove that tofu is neither boring nor flavorless. However, if all my efforts have failed to turn you into a tofu fan, I have one last solution: mapo tofu, a classic Chinese dish from the Sichuan province. Trust me, its spicy kick and deep umami flavors will make you wonder why you ever doubted tofu in the first place.

Kosher salt, to taste
10½ oz (300g) silken tofu (or soft tofu), cut into ½-inch (1.25cm) cubes
1 tbsp neutral-tasting oil
1½ tbsp chili oil (or neutral-tasting oil)
4⅓ oz (130g) ground pork
2 green onions, thinly sliced, white and green parts divided
2 garlic cloves, finely chopped
1 tsp freshly grated ginger
¼ red bell pepper, diced
¼ green bell pepper, diced
½ tbsp Sichuan peppercorn oil (or 1 tsp toasted ground Sichuan peppercorns)
½ tsp Chinese black vinegar (or white vinegar, rice vinegar)
1 tbsp cornstarch
1 tbsp water
1 tsp toasted sesame oil

FOR THE SAUCE

1 tbsp Chinese chili bean paste (doubanjiang)
½ tbsp soy sauce
1 tbsp oyster sauce
1 tbsp Shaoxing wine (or mirin, dry sherry, water, etc.)
1 tsp granulated sugar
Pinch of MSG (optional)

FOR THE CHICKEN STOCK

1 cup water
½ tbsp chicken bouillon powder

1. To make the sauce, in a small bowl, stir together all ingredients until fully incorporated. Set aside.
2. To make the chicken stock, in a medium bowl, stir together all ingredients until fully incorporated. Set aside.
3. Bring a pot of water to a boil. Add a pinch of salt. Blanch the tofu for 2 minutes or until the tofu is warm. Drain and set aside.
4. In a large wok or pan, add the oil and chili oil and heat over medium heat. Once it gets nice and hot, add the ground pork. Break up the pork and cook for 3 minutes or until the fat has rendered.
5. Add the white parts of the green onions, garlic, and ginger, and sauté for 30 seconds or until fragrant. Increase the heat to high, add the sauce, and cook for 1 minute. Add the bell peppers and stir-fry for 30 seconds or until everything is coated.
6. Add the chicken stock and bring it to a boil. Add the drained tofu and gently mix around. Simmer for 2 to 3 minutes. (Do not stir vigorously or the tofu will break apart.) Add the Sichuan peppercorn oil and vinegar and gently stir together.
7. In a small bowl, mix the cornstarch with the water. Add the slurry to the wok and immediately stir until the sauce is thickened and shiny, about 1 minute. Turn the heat off. Add the sesame oil and give a final mix.
8. Transfer to a serving bowl or plate. Garnish with the green parts of the green onions. Serve with hot rice.

CLAIRE SAYS:

This Aaron-style mapo tofu may not be a perfectly traditional Sichuan recipe, but after eating hundreds of bowls, I can confidently say I've rarely tasted one better than this. And the best part? It's incredibly easy to make. No, I'm not just saying this because I'm his wife. Trust me—give it a try, and you'll see what I mean.

CLAIRE SAYS:

The fantastic flavor of kung pao chicken comes from the perfect combination of evenly cut chicken pieces, a variety of vegetables, and the delightful crunch of peanuts. The crispiness of roasted peanuts is truly the highlight. If you're not a big fan of peanuts or have allergies, don't worry about it—simply substitute them with another type of nut. My personal recommendation? Cashews!

KUNG PAO CHICKEN

Spicy Stir-Fried Chicken with Peanuts

PREP TIME: **20 minutes + 20 minutes to marinate** // COOK TIME: **10 minutes** // SERVES: **3**

There are some dishes you may not want to pay for and have at restaurants, like PB&J sandwiches, mac and cheese, or a simple salad. Who wants to pay $15 to $20 for that, right? For me, that dish is kung pao chicken. It's made with inexpensive ingredients and the preparation is simple. By making it at home, you can feed the entire family an incredibly delicious meal for the price of just one serving at a restaurant.

---

12 oz (350g) boneless skinless chicken breasts (or thighs), cut into ½-inch (1.25cm) cubes
3 tbsp neutral-tasting oil, divided
½ cup unsalted peanuts
2 to 3 dried chilies, cut into small pieces *(for less heat, remove the seeds)*
3 garlic cloves, finely chopped
2 tsp freshly grated ginger
¼ green bell pepper (optional), cut into ½-inch (1.25cm) pieces
¼ red bell pepper (optional), cut into ½-inch (1.25cm) pieces
4 green onions, cut into ½-inch (1.25cm) pieces
1 tsp Sichuan peppercorn oil (or ½ tsp toasted ground Sichuan peppercorns)

FOR THE MARINADE

1 tsp soy sauce
1 tsp Shaoxing wine (or mirin, dry sherry, water, etc.)
¼ tsp white pepper (or black pepper)
1 tbsp neutral-tasting oil
1 tbsp cornstarch

FOR THE SAUCE

1 tbsp soy sauce
½ tbsp oyster sauce
½ tbsp Chinese chili bean paste (doubanjiang)
1 tbsp granulated sugar
1½ tbsp Chinese black vinegar (or white vinegar, rice vinegar)
1 tsp Shaoxing wine (or mirin, dry sherry, water, etc.)
½ tsp chicken bouillon powder
½ tbsp cornstarch
3 tbsp water

1. In a large bowl, combine the marinade ingredients and coat the chicken in the marinade. Cover with plastic wrap and marinate in the fridge for at least 20 minutes.
2. To prepare the sauce, in a small bowl, whisk together all the ingredients until thoroughly combined. Set aside.
3. In a large wok or pan, heat 2 tablespoons of oil over medium heat. Once it gets nice and hot, add the peanuts. Roast for 2 to 3 minutes or until deep dark brown. Stir constantly to prevent burning. Remove from the wok, leaving the oil behind.
4. Place the same wok over high heat. Once it's heated, add the marinated chicken in a single layer. Let sear for 1 minute or until golden brown on the bottom. Flip and cook for 2 to 3 minutes or until cooked through. Remove from the wok and set aside.
5. In the same wok, add 1 tablespoon of oil and heat over medium heat. Add the dried chilies and cook for 30 seconds or until they start to brown. Add the garlic and ginger and stir-fry for 30 seconds or until fragrant.
6. Add the chicken back into the wok and increase the heat to high. Give the sauce a quick stir and add it to the wok. Stir-fry for 30 seconds or until the sauce has thickened and become shiny.
7. Add the bell peppers (if using), green onions, and peanuts. Stir-fry for 1 more minute. Turn off the heat. Add the Sichuan peppercorn oil and give a final mix. Transfer to a serving plate. Serve with hot rice.

MONGOLIAN BEEF

Sweet and Savory Stir-Fried Beef

PREP TIME: **15 minutes + 20 minutes to marinate** // COOK TIME: **10 minutes** // SERVES: **3–4**

If I had to choose just one dish from American-style Chinese food, it would definitely be Mongolian beef. Why? Because this dish perfectly proves the absolute truth: More green onion, more delicious! Crispy, tender beef coated in a sweet and savory sauce, paired with a generous amount of green onions—this dish is nothing short of perfection.

---

1 lb (450g) beef flank steak, sliced against the grain into ¼-inch (0.5cm) thick slices
½ cup cornstarch
1 cup high-heat oil (such as canola, avocado, vegetable, etc.), for frying
4 green onions, the tops cut into 2-inch (5cm) pieces, plus thinly sliced white parts
5 garlic cloves, finely chopped
2 tsp freshly grated ginger
4 dried red chilies (optional)
½ tbsp toasted sesame oil

FOR THE MARINADE

½ tbsp soy sauce
½ tbsp Shaoxing wine (or mirin, dry sherry, water, etc.)
¼ tsp white pepper (or black pepper)
¼ tsp baking soda
1 tbsp cornstarch
1 tbsp neutral-tasting oil

FOR THE SAUCE

3 tbsp soy sauce
1 tbsp oyster sauce
½ tsp dark soy sauce
1½ tbsp granulated sugar
1 tbsp honey
1 tbsp Shaoxing wine (or mirin, dry sherry, water, etc.)
Black pepper, to taste
1 tsp cornstarch
1 tbsp water

1. In a large bowl, combine the marinade ingredients and toss the beef pieces in the marinade until evenly coated. Cover with plastic wrap and marinate in the fridge for at least 20 minutes.
2. To prepare the sauce, in a small bowl, whisk together all the ingredients until thoroughly combined. Set aside.
3. Lightly coat the marinated beef pieces with the cornstarch until thoroughly coated.
4. In a large wok or pan, heat the oil over high heat. When it gets nice and hot, just before the oil starts to smoke, add the beef pieces in batches and shallow-fry for 2 minutes or until the beef is crispy and golden brown. Remove the fried beef from the oil and place on a wire rack to drain.
5. Strain the oil through a fine mesh strainer, leaving 2 tablespoons in the wok. Heat the oil over medium heat. Add the white parts of the green onions, garlic, ginger, and dried chilies (if using), and sauté for 1 minute or until fragrant. Give the sauce a quick stir and add it to the wok. Bring to a boil.
6. Once the sauce starts bubbling, increase the heat to high, add the beef, and toss together for 30 seconds or until the beef is thoroughly coated. Turn off the heat. Add the green parts of the green onions and sesame oil. Give a final mix. Transfer to a serving plate. Serve with hot rice.

CLAIRE SAYS:

Mongolian beef is usually served with hot rice, as they complement each other perfectly. However, it also pairs well with noodles—what we like to call Mongolian beef noodles. While this variation isn't included in this book, don't worry! You can find the recipe on our YouTube channel and blog. Trust me, it will be the best twist on Mongolian beef you'll ever taste.

CLAIRE SAYS:

Whenever Aaron says he's making chow mein, I always ask him to use chicken thighs. The fat rendered from the chicken blends beautifully with the sauce and coats the noodles, creating an incredibly rich and deep flavor. If you're not on a diet, I highly recommend giving it a try!

CHICKEN CHOW MEIN

Stir-Fried Noodles with Chicken

PREP TIME: **15 minutes + 10 minutes to marinate** // COOK TIME: **15 minutes** // SERVES: **3–4**

Forget about greasy, flavorless, pre-made takeout chow mein. When you cook this at home with some proper technique, you'll unlock a whole new level of taste and flavor in freshly made chow mein. Get ready to taste the difference!

---

7 oz (200g) boneless skin-on chicken thighs (or breasts), cut into thin strips
7 oz (200g) dried egg noodles (or spaghetti noodles)
4 tbsp neutral-tasting oil, divided
3 garlic cloves, finely chopped
½ yellow onion, thinly sliced
4½ oz (130g) green cabbage, thinly sliced
½ red bell pepper, julienned
⅓ carrot (60g), cut into thin matchsticks
2 green onions, cut into 2-inch (5cm) pieces
1 tsp toasted sesame oil

FOR THE MARINADE

1 tsp soy sauce
Small pinch of granulated sugar
½ egg white
1½ tbsp cornstarch

FOR THE CHOW MEIN SAUCE

2½ tbsp soy sauce
½ tbsp dark soy sauce
2 tbsp oyster sauce
1½ tbsp Shaoxing wine (or mirin, dry sherry, water, etc.)
1 tsp granulated sugar
¼ tsp white pepper (or black pepper)
Small pinch of MSG (optional)

1. In a large bowl, combine all the marinade ingredients and toss the chicken pieces in the marinade until evenly coated. Cover with plastic wrap and marinate in the fridge for at least 10 minutes.
2. To make the chow mein sauce, in a small bowl, whisk together all the ingredients until thoroughly combined. Set aside.
3. Cook the noodles in a pot of water according to the package instructions. Once they are cooked through, rinse under cold water and drain well. Set aside.
4. In a large wok or pan, heat 3 tablespoons of oil over high heat. Once it gets nice and hot, add the marinated chicken and cook for 2 to 3 minutes or until nicely browned. When the chicken is cooked through, remove from the wok and set aside.
5. Place the same wok over medium heat, add the garlic and onion, and sauté for 30 seconds or until fragrant. Increase the heat to high. Add the cabbage, bell pepper, carrot, and green onions, and stir-fry for 2 minutes or until the vegetables are slightly cooked. Remove from the wok and set aside.
6. Place the same wok over medium-high heat and add 1 tablespoon of oil. When it gets nice and hot, add the noodles in a single layer and toast for 1 to 2 minutes or until the noodles are nicely browned on the bottom.
7. Increase the heat to high. Add half of the chow mein sauce along with the cooked vegetables and chicken. Stir-fry for 1 minute or until everything is well distributed. Add the remaining sauce and stir-fry for 2 minutes or until everything is evenly coated with the sauce.
8. Turn off the heat. Drizzle with the sesame oil and stir to combine. Transfer to a serving plate and serve immediately.

BEEF LO MEIN

Stir-Fried Soft Noodles with Beef

PREP TIME: **15 minutes + 10 minutes to marinate** // COOK TIME: **15 minutes** // SERVES: **4**

Deciding between chow mein and lo mein can be one of life's toughest choices. Both dishes are iconic and delicious Chinese noodle options. However, if you prefer noodles that are saucier and more tender, the answer is clear. With melt-in-your-mouth beef, plenty of vegetables, and a flavorful sauce, this beef lo mein is sure to become a weeknight staple in your household.

10⅓ oz (300g) beef flank steak, thinly sliced against the grain
1 lb (450g) fresh or frozen lo mein noodles (or 8 oz [225g] dried spaghetti noodles)
3 tbsp neutral-tasting oil, divided
3 garlic cloves, finely chopped
1 tsp freshly grated ginger
⅓ carrot (60g), cut into thin matchsticks
½ yellow onion, thinly sliced
2 baby bok choy, cut into bite-sized pieces
⅓ red bell pepper, julienned
2 green onions, cut into 2-inch (5cm) pieces
1 tsp toasted sesame oil

FOR THE MARINADE

½ tbsp soy sauce
¼ tsp white pepper (or black pepper)
Small pinch of granulated sugar
¼ tsp baking soda
1 tbsp Shaoxing wine (or mirin, dry sherry, water, etc.)
½ tbsp cornstarch
1 tbsp neutral-tasting oil

FOR THE LO MEIN SAUCE

½ cup water
½ tbsp chicken bouillon powder
2 tbsp soy sauce
½ tbsp dark soy sauce
2 tbsp oyster sauce
1 tsp granulated sugar
1 tbsp Shaoxing wine (or mirin, dry sherry, water, etc.)
¼ tsp white pepper (or black pepper)
1 tbsp cornstarch
Small pinch of MSG (optional)

1. In a large bowl, combine all the marinade ingredients and toss the beef pieces in the marinade until evenly coated. Cover with plastic wrap and marinate in the fridge for at least 10 minutes.
2. To make the lo mein sauce, in a small bowl, combine all the ingredients. Mix until thoroughly combined and set aside.
3. Cook the noodles in a pot of water according to the package instructions. Once the noodles are cooked through, rinse under cold water and drain well. Set aside.
4. In a large wok or pan, heat 1 tablespoon of oil over high heat. Once it gets nice and hot, add the marinated beef and cook for 2 to 3 minutes or until nicely browned. Remove from the wok and set aside.
5. Place the same wok over medium-high heat and add 2 tablespoons of oil. When it gets nice and hot, add the garlic and ginger, and sauté for 30 seconds or until fragrant.
6. Add the carrot, onion, bok choy, bell pepper, and green onions. Stir-fry for 1 to 2 minutes or until the vegetables are slightly cooked.
7. Reduce the heat to medium. Add the drained noodles and stir-fry for 1 minute. Add the beef and the lo mein sauce. Give a good stir for 2 to 3 minutes or until the sauce is thickened and everything is nicely coated with the sauce.
8. Turn off the heat. Drizzle with the sesame oil and give a final mix. Transfer to a serving plate and serve immediately.

CLAIRE SAYS:

In Korea, it's quite difficult to find precooked or uncooked lo mein noodles. That's why we often use spaghetti noodles as a substitute. If you're using spaghetti just like us, make sure to cook them a little longer than al dente. This will help you achieve a texture that is closer to store-bought lo mein noodles.

CLAIRE SAYS:

If you want to add a twist and enjoy even crispier and juicier chicken, consider using the batter from a Korean fried chicken recipe (page 56). You'll discover an incredible variation of orange chicken that's absolutely worth a try!

ORANGE CHICKEN

Crispy Fried Chicken with Orange Sauce

PREP TIME: **15 minutes + 10 minutes to marinate** // COOK TIME: **20 minutes** // SERVES: **3–4**

I love orange chicken. Crispy fried chicken and a slightly sweet and tangy orange sauce, along with various aromatic spices, create the perfect flavor combination. But there has always been one problem when I order this dish as takeout: the texture. The nature of pre-made takeout food often means sacrificing that perfect crispiness. But don't worry about it. When you make it at home, that problem will disappear. This homemade version will prove to be better than anything you can find at a restaurant.

---

17 oz (500g) boneless, skinless chicken breasts (or thighs), cut into bite-sized pieces
1 cup potato starch (or cornstarch)
2 tbsp neutral-tasting oil, plus more for frying
4 garlic cloves, finely chopped
3 tsp freshly grated ginger
1 mild red chili pepper (optional), thinly sliced
1 tbsp cornstarch
1 tbsp water
½ tsp toasted sesame oil
Generous pinch of toasted sesame seeds
1 green onion, thinly sliced

FOR THE MARINADE

½ tbsp soy sauce
1 tbsp Shaoxing wine (or mirin, dry sherry, water, etc.)
Freshly cracked black pepper, to taste

FOR THE ORANGE CHICKEN SAUCE

¼ cup granulated sugar
¼ cup white vinegar (or rice vinegar)
¼ cup fresh orange juice
1½ tbsp soy sauce
1 tbsp oyster sauce
4 tbsp store-bought orange juice
1 tsp orange zest

1. In a large bowl, combine all the marinade ingredients and toss the chicken pieces in the marinade until evenly coated. Cover with plastic wrap and marinate in the fridge for at least 10 minutes.
2. To make the orange chicken sauce, in a small bowl, combine all the ingredients. Mix until thoroughly combined and set aside.
3. Add the potato starch (or cornstarch) to a big tray. Grab a piece of chicken and lightly coat the outside. Place the chicken piece on another tray. Repeat with the remaining chicken pieces.
4. In a large wok or heavy-bottomed pot, heat about 2 inches (5cm) of cooking oil to 340°F (170°C). Working in batches, carefully place the chicken pieces in the oil (dropping them away from you). Fry for 3 to 4 minutes or until light brown. Remove from the hot oil and place on a wire rack. Using a fine sieve, remove little bits that are left in the oil.
5. Increase the oil temperature to 355°F (180°C). Fry the chicken pieces a second time for 2 to 3 minutes until crispy and cooked through. Transfer to the wire rack and rest.
6. In another large wok or pan, heat 2 tablespoons of oil over medium heat. Once it gets nice and hot, add the garlic, ginger, and chili pepper (if using). Sauté for 1 minute or until the garlic just starts to go brown. Add the orange chicken sauce and bring to a boil.
7. In a small bowl, mix the cornstarch and water. Once the sauce comes to a boil, add the slurry to the wok and immediately stir until the sauce is thickened and shiny. Add the chicken and quickly toss together for 1 minute or until nicely coated.
8. Turn off the heat. Drizzle with the sesame oil and give a final mix. Transfer to a serving plate and garnish with toasted sesame seeds and green onion. Serve immediately.

NOTE: In Step 5, the oil can make a lot more noise and bubbles than during the first fry, but don't worry about it. That's natural. This double-frying technique will help remove all of the moisture from the crust and make it extra crispy.

DAN DAN NOODLES

Spicy Sichuan Noodles with Pork and Sesame Sauce

PREP TIME: **7 minutes + 10 minutes to marinate** // COOK TIME: **15 minutes** // SERVES: **2**

Dan dan noodles is a classic Chinese dish from the Sichuan province. Since it's super famous, there are so many great recipes out there, but as always, my version will be the simplest but most delicious homemade dan dan noodles that you've ever had. I guarantee it!

---

12 oz (350g) ground pork
1 tbsp neutral-tasting oil
2 green onions, thinly sliced, white and green parts divided
3 garlic cloves, finely chopped
1 tsp freshly grated ginger
¼ cup preserved mustard greens (yacai)
2 servings white wheat noodles (or spaghetti noodles)
2 baby bok choy, quartered lengthwise

FOR THE MARINADE

1 tbsp soy sauce
Small pinch of granulated sugar
Kosher salt, to taste
Freshly cracked black pepper, to taste
1 tbsp Shaoxing wine (or mirin, dry sherry, water, etc.)

FOR THE SAUCE

1½ tbsp soy sauce
½ tsp dark soy sauce
2 tbsp Chinese sesame paste
½ tbsp chicken bouillon powder
1 tbsp Chinese black vinegar (or white vinegar, rice vinegar)
1 tsp granulated sugar
1 tsp finely ground toasted Sichuan peppercorns (or Sichuan peppercorn oil)
2 tbsp chili oil (see note), plus more to drizzle
Small pinch of MSG (optional)

1. In a large bowl, combine all the marinade ingredients, add the pork and mix until thoroughly combined. Cover with plastic wrap and marinate in the fridge for at least 10 minutes.
2. To make the sauce, in a medium bowl, whisk together all the ingredients until thoroughly combined. Set aside.
3. In a large wok or pan, heat the oil over medium-high heat. Once it gets nice and hot, add the marinated pork. Break up the pork and cook for 3 minutes or until it is no longer pink.
4. Add the white parts of the green onions, garlic, ginger, and preserved mustard greens. Stir-fry for 3 minutes or until the pork is cooked through. Set aside.
5. Bring a pot of water to a boil. Once boiling, cook the noodles according to the package instructions. Once the noodles are cooked, reserve ½ cup noodle cooking water and take out the noodles. Set aside.
6. In the same water, blanch the bok choy for 30 seconds to 1 minute. Set aside.
7. To serve, in each serving bowl, add half of the sauce and ¼ cup of noodle cooking water. Give them a good stir. Divide the noodles evenly between the bowls. Top with some pork topping, bok choy, and the green parts of the green onions. Drizzle with chili oil for an extra kick. Enjoy immediately.

NOTE: Quick and easy homemade chili oil recipe
4 tbsp Korean chili pepper flakes (gochugaru)
1 tbsp finely chopped garlic
¼ cup sliced white parts of green onions
1 cup neutral-tasting oil

1. In a heat-proof container, stir together all the ingredients. Microwave, uncovered, for 3 minutes.
2. Once it's completely cooled down, you can keep it in the fridge for 1 month.

CLAIRE SAYS:

If you're a big fan of spicy food, feel free to add more chili oil or Sichuan peppercorn powder before mixing the noodles. The beauty of this dish is that you can adjust the spice level to suit your taste.

CLAIRE SAYS:

This recipe uses baking soda to tenderize the beef, making it ideal for more affordable cuts. However, if you choose higher-quality steak cuts, you'll enjoy more tender and juicier beef and broccoli. So feel free to play around with other cuts to discover your personal favorite. For your information, Aaron and I personally love using chuck flap tail.

BEEF AND BROCCOLI

Stir-Fried Beef with Broccoli

PREP TIME: **15 minutes + 20 minutes to marinate** // COOK TIME: **15 minutes** // SERVES: **3–4**

Tender, juicy beef smothered in a glossy, savory sauce and paired with perfectly crisp broccoli—it's a combination that's hard to resist! However, when you make this at home with some random online recipes, you may find yourself disappointed because the flavors don't quite match the magic of a restaurant meal. But don't worry about it! This recipe will bring restaurant-quality beef and broccoli straight to your table. Get ready to impress your taste buds!

---

17 oz (500g) flank steak, sliced against the grain into ¼-inch (0.5cm) thick slices
Kosher salt, to taste
1 head broccoli, about 9 oz (250g) in total, cut into bite-sized florets
3 tbsp neutral-tasting oil, divided
4 garlic cloves, finely chopped
2 tsp freshly grated ginger
2 green onions, thinly sliced, white and green parts divided
⅓ carrot (60g), thinly sliced
1 tsp toasted sesame oil

FOR THE MARINADE

1 tbsp soy sauce
1 tbsp Shaoxing wine (or mirin, dry sherry, water, etc.)
¼ tsp white pepper (or black pepper)
1 tbsp cornstarch
¼ tsp baking soda
1 tbsp neutral-tasting oil

FOR THE BEEF AND BROCCOLI SAUCE

1 tbsp soy sauce
2 tbsp oyster sauce
½ tsp dark soy sauce
1 tbsp granulated sugar
1 tbsp Shaoxing wine (or mirin, dry sherry, water, etc.)
1 tsp chicken bouillon powder
5 tbsp water
1 tbsp cornstarch
Small pinch of MSG (optional)

1. In a large bowl, combine all the marinade ingredients and toss the beef in the marinade until thoroughly coated. Cover with plastic wrap and marinate in the fridge for at least 20 minutes.
2. To make the beef and broccoli sauce, in a small bowl, combine all the ingredients. Mix until thoroughly combined and set aside.
3. Bring a pot of water to a boil with a pinch of salt. Once boiling, blanch the broccoli for 1 minute. Shock them in some ice water. Drain and set aside.
4. In a large wok or pan, heat 1 tablespoon of oil over high heat. Once it gets nice and hot, add the marinated beef in a single layer. Sear for 1 minute or until the beef is nicely browned on the bottom. Flip and sear on the other side for another 1 to 2 minutes or until the beef is cooked. Remove from the wok and set aside.
5. To the same wok, add 2 tablespoons of oil and heat over medium heat. Once it gets nice and hot, add the garlic, ginger, and white parts of the green onions, and sauté for 1 minute or until fragrant.
6. Increase the heat to medium-high. Add the carrot and broccoli and stir-fry for 1 minute or until the vegetables are coated with the aromatic oil.
7. Increase the heat to high. Add the beef back in and toss together for 1 minute. Add in the sauce and give a good stir for 1 to 2 minutes or until the sauce becomes thickened and shiny.
8. Turn off the heat. Add the sesame oil and the green parts of the green onions and give a final mix. Transfer to a serving plate and serve with hot rice.

BEIJING BEEF

Crispy Beef with Tangy and Sweet Sauce

PREP TIME: **15 minutes + 20 minutes to marinate** // COOK TIME: **15 minutes** // SERVES: **3–4**

Yet another insanely delicious beef stir-fry dish. However, I truly don't understand why it seems to be somewhat underrated. It's so simple and delicious, it just doesn't make sense. If anyone knows why, please let me know. Anyway, juicy, tender beef tossed in a slightly sweet, spicy, and tangy sauce—trust me, the moment you take a bite, you'll regret not having tried it sooner.

---

17 oz (500g) flank steak, sliced against the grain into ¼-inch (0.5cm) thick slices
1 egg white
1 cup cornstarch
2 tbsp neutral-tasting oil, plus more for frying
½ yellow onion, cut into bite-sized pieces
1 red bell pepper, cut into bite-sized pieces
7 garlic cloves, finely chopped
2 tsp freshly grated ginger

FOR THE MARINADE

½ tbsp soy sauce
1 tbsp Shaoxing wine (or mirin, dry sherry, water, etc.)
½ tsp white pepper (or black pepper)
¼ tsp baking soda

FOR THE BEIJING BEEF SAUCE

½ tbsp soy sauce
2½ tbsp oyster sauce
½ tsp dark soy sauce
1 tbsp white vinegar (or rice vinegar)
1 tbsp Chinese black vinegar (or white vinegar, rice vinegar)
1 tbsp Shaoxing wine (or mirin, dry sherry, water, etc.)
2 tbsp ketchup
1½ tbsp granulated sugar
1 tbsp sambal (or sriracha)
7 tbsp water
1 tbsp cornstarch
Small pinch of MSG (optional)

1. In a large bowl, combine all the marinade ingredients and toss the beef in the marinade until thoroughly coated. Cover with plastic wrap and marinate in the fridge for at least 20 minutes.
2. To make the Beijing beef sauce, in a small bowl, combine all the ingredients. Mix until thoroughly combined and set aside.
3. To the beef, add the egg white and gently massage it. Add the cornstarch to a big tray. Grab a piece of beef and lightly coat the outside. Place the beef piece on another tray. Repeat with the remaining beef pieces.
4. In a large wok or heavy-bottomed pot, heat about 2 inches (5cm) of cooking oil to 355°F (180°C). Working in batches, carefully place the beef pieces in the oil (dropping them away from you). Fry for 2 to 3 minutes or until light golden brown. Remove from the hot oil and place on a wire rack.
5. In another wok or pan, add 2 tablespoons of oil and heat over medium-high heat. Once it gets nice and hot, add the onion, bell pepper, garlic, and ginger. Sauté for 1 to 2 minutes or until the onion starts to soften.
6. Add the Beijing beef sauce, give it a good stir, and simmer for 30 seconds or until the sauce is thickened. Add in the beef and toss together for 1 minute or until the beef pieces are nicely coated. Turn off the heat. Transfer to a serving plate and serve with hot rice.

CLAIRE SAYS:

The sweet, spicy, and tangy Beijing beef sauce pairs wonderfully with rice, so instead of serving the rice separately in a bowl, try plating the rice first and then generously layering the Beijing beef on top. This will not only make your dish look more visually appealing but also enhance the overall flavor experience.

CLAIRE SAYS:

If you're a big fan of eggs like me, I recommend adding some hard-boiled eggs about 10 minutes before finishing Step 5. The flavorful red braising sauce will soak into the eggs, providing a delightful experience that is quite different from the pork belly itself.

HONG SHAO ROU

Pork Belly Braised in Soy Sauce

PREP TIME: **10 minutes** // COOK TIME: **1 hour 45 minutes** // SERVES: **6–7**

If you've been dreaming of an incredibly tender meat dish that will change your life, your wish is about to come true. This beloved Chinese classic features juicy, tender, and aromatic braised pork belly that is sure to elevate your culinary experience.

---

4 lb (1.8kg) skin-on pork belly, cut into 2-inch (5cm) cubes
2 tbsp neutral-tasting oil
3 tbsp granulated sugar
3 garlic cloves, smashed
5 slices fresh ginger (about 35g)
2–3 green onions, cut into 2-inch (5cm) pieces, plus more to garnish
4 whole star anise
2 bay leaves
1 small cinnamon stick
1 tsp Sichuan peppercorns
6 tbsp Shaoxing wine
3 tbsp soy sauce
1 tbsp oyster sauce
1 tbsp dark soy sauce
1 tbsp chicken bouillon powder
5 cups hot water
1 English cucumber (optional), thinly sliced, to garnish

1. Bring a pot of water to a boil. Once boiling, carefully add the pork belly and blanch for 4 to 5 minutes to remove any impurities from the pork. Drain it in a colander, give a quick rinse, and drain again.
2. In a large wok or pan, heat the oil over medium-high heat. Once it's heated, add the pork pieces and get some sear on all sides, about 10 minutes. If your wok or pan is not large enough for all the pork, do this in batches.
3. Once the pork gets light golden brown and the fat has rendered out, reduce the heat to medium. Add the sugar and give a good stir for 2 minutes. (The traditional method involves melting rock sugar in oil to create a syrup that coats the pork belly. However, to make it easier and simpler, this recipe uses granulated sugar. This is a shortcut version of caramelizing rock sugar, so be sure to keep stirring and to evenly coat the outside of the pork.)
4. Add the garlic, ginger, green onions, star anise, bay leaves, cinnamon stick, and Sichuan peppercorns, and stir for 1 minute. Add the Shaoxing wine, soy sauce, oyster sauce, dark soy sauce, and chicken bouillon powder. Give a good stir for 3 minutes or until everything is combined thoroughly.
5. Turn off the heat. Transfer everything into a large pot with hot water. Simmer over medium-low, covered, for 80 minutes or until the pork is fork-tender, stirring every 10 minutes.
6. After the pork has simmered for 80 minutes, increase the heat to medium-high and stir constantly until the liquid has almost evaporated. When the sauce gets thicker and glossy and the pork is nicely coated, turn the heat off. Transfer to a serving plate and garnish with sliced cucumber (if using) and green onions. Serve with hot rice. Enjoy!

GREEN ONION OIL NOODLES

Noodle Stir-Fry with Green Onion Oil

PREP TIME: **5 minutes** // COOK TIME: **5 minutes** // SERVES: **2**

Here's yet another incredibly simple noodle dish with an ingredient we love: green onions. Essentially, it's just green onions, basic seasonings, and noodles—but it beautifully showcases the magic of simplicity.

---

2 servings white wheat noodles (or spaghetti noodles)
4 tbsp neutral-tasting oil
4–5 green onions, thinly sliced, plus more to garnish
2 tbsp soy sauce
1 tbsp oyster sauce
1 tsp dark soy sauce (optional)
½ tbsp granulated sugar
Kosher salt, to taste
½ cup cilantro, roughly chopped
2 crispy fried eggs (optional), to serve

1. Bring a pot of water to a boil. Once boiling, cook the noodles according to the package instructions.
2. Meanwhile, in a large wok or pan, heat the oil over medium-high heat. Once it gets nice and hot, add the green onions and sauté for 3 to 4 minutes or until light brown and fragrant.
3. Add the cooked noodles, soy sauce, oyster sauce, dark soy sauce (if using), and sugar. Increase the heat to high. Toss thoroughly until the noodles are evenly coated with the green onion oil and the seasonings.
4. Turn off the heat. Taste and add salt if needed. Plate and top with cilantro and fried eggs (if using). Enjoy immediately.

CLAIRE SAYS:
More green onions = more delicious! That's the only tip that I can give you.

CLAIRE SAYS:

As you probably know, I'm not the biggest fan of cilantro, but I have to admit—this dish tastes better with it. My apologies to the members of the "I hate cilantro" club.

SESAME NOODLES

Noodles Tossed in Creamy Sesame Sauce

PREP TIME: **10 minutes** // COOK TIME: **5 minutes** // SERVES: **2**

Spending a lot of time and effort doesn't always guarantee a better taste. You don't believe it? Then give these sesame noodles a try. These creamy, savory, and nutty noodles will prove it.

---

2 servings Chinese dried knife-sliced noodles (or spaghetti noodles)
1 English cucumber, julienned
1–2 green onions, thinly sliced
½ cup cilantro (optional), roughly chopped
Soft-boiled eggs (optional), to serve
3 tbsp toasted sesame seeds, ground

FOR THE SESAME NOODLE SAUCE

2 tbsp Chinese sesame paste (or peanut butter)
2 tbsp soy sauce
1 tsp dark soy sauce
2 tbsp Chinese black vinegar (or white vinegar, rice vinegar)
1 tsp granulated sugar
1 tsp freshly grated ginger
2 tbsp chili oil (see note)
½ tbsp chicken bouillon powder
2 garlic cloves, finely chopped

1. Bring a pot of water to a boil. Once boiling, cook the noodles according to the package instructions. Once the noodles are cooked, reserve ¼ cup of noodle cooking water and drain the noodles. Set aside.
2. Meanwhile, to make the sesame noodle sauce, in a large bowl, combine all the ingredients and the reserved noodle cooking water. Mix until thoroughly combined.
3. Add the noodles to the sauce. Toss together until thoroughly combined.
4. Divide the noodles evenly between two serving plates. Top with cucumber, green onions, cilantro (if using), soft-boiled eggs (if using), and ground sesame seeds. Enjoy immediately!

NOTE: Quick and easy homemade chili oil recipe

4 tbsp Korean chili pepper flakes (gochugaru)
1 tbsp finely chopped garlic
¼ cup sliced white parts of green onions
1 cup neutral-tasting oil

1. In a small heatproof container, stir together all the ingredients. Microwave, uncovered, for 3 minutes.
2. Once it's completely cooled down, you can keep it in the fridge for 1 month.

TOFU AND BROCCOLI

Stir-Fried Tofu with Broccoli

PREP TIME: **15 minutes** // COOK TIME: **15 minutes** // SERVES: **2–3**

Surprisingly, a lot of our meat-loving subscribers have told us this dish changed the way they see vegetable dishes. Crispy fried tofu and vibrant green broccoli in a savory, flavorful, and glossy sauce—this is truly one of the best Chinese dishes of all time. Once you try it, trust me, it might just become your favorite vegetable dish ever.

Kosher salt, to taste
1 head broccoli, about 9 oz (250g) in total, cut into bite-sized florets
18 oz (520g) firm tofu (or extra firm tofu), cut into 1-inch (2.5cm) cubes and patted dry
Freshly cracked black pepper, to taste
½ cup cornstarch (or potato starch)
4 tbsp neutral-tasting oil, divided
5 garlic cloves, finely chopped
2 tsp freshly grated ginger
2 green onions, thinly sliced, white and green parts divided
½ tbsp toasted sesame oil
1 mild red chili pepper (optional), for color
Generous pinch of toasted sesame seeds, to garnish

FOR THE TOFU AND BROCCOLI SAUCE

1 tbsp soy sauce
2 tbsp oyster sauce
½ tsp dark soy sauce
1 tbsp granulated sugar
1 tbsp Shaoxing wine (or mirin, dry sherry, water, etc.)
1 tsp chicken bouillon powder
½ cup water
1 tbsp cornstarch
Small pinch of MSG (optional)

1. To make the tofu and broccoli sauce, in a small bowl, combine all the ingredients. Mix until thoroughly combined and set aside.
2. Bring a pot of water to a boil with a pinch of salt. Once boiling, blanch the broccoli for 1 minute. Shock them in some ice water. Drain and set aside.
3. Lightly season the tofu with salt and pepper. Add the cornstarch (or potato starch) to a big tray. Grab some tofu cubes and lightly coat them in the cornstarch. Repeat with the remaining tofu.
4. In a large wok or pan, heat 3 tablespoons of oil over medium heat. Once heated, add in the tofu and fry for 6 to 7 minutes or until light golden brown. (Tofu cubes tend to stick together, so I recommend working in 2 batches.) Remove from the wok and set aside.
5. To the same wok, add 1 tablespoon of oil and heat over medium-high heat. Once heated, add the garlic, ginger, and white parts of the green onions, and sauté for 1 minute or until fragrant.
6. Add the tofu and broccoli sauce and stir for 1 minute or until the sauce has thickened. Add the tofu and broccoli and toss together for 1 minute or until everything is nicely coated.
7. Turn off the heat. Drizzle with the sesame oil and give a final mix. Transfer to a serving plate. Garnish with the green parts of the green onions, chili pepper (if using), and toasted sesame seeds. Serve with hot rice.

CLAIRE SAYS:

Every time Aaron talks about tofu dishes, he always says, "This dish will make even tofu haters ..." But I think the true star of this dish is the broccoli. The crunchy broccoli stir-fried in an aromatic and savory sauce is irresistible to anyone in the world.

CLAIRE SAYS:

If you're eager to try this dish but feel a bit intimidated by deep-frying, you can simply go with pan-frying or shallow-frying instead. While you may need to compromise a bit on flavor and texture, it will still turn out absolutely delicious. So don't worry about it and give it a try!

SESAME CHICKEN

Crispy Fried Chicken with Sweet Sesame Sauce

PREP TIME: **15 minutes + 10 minutes to marinate** // COOK TIME: **15 minutes** // SERVES: **3–4**

Sesame chicken is not only the greatest chicken dish in the fried chicken world but also one of our family's all-time favorite Chinese-American dishes. For that reason, every time we visited a Chinese restaurant, this dish was always on our table. Every time we left the restaurant, we promised to try something new next time, but somehow this crispy, juicy fried chicken coated in a sweet and savory sauce always found its way back to our table. It's just that irresistible!

---

1 lb (450g) boneless, skin-on or skinless chicken thighs (or breasts), cut into bite-sized pieces
1 cup potato starch (or cornstarch)
2 tbsp neutral-tasting oil, plus more for frying
3 garlic cloves, finely chopped
2 tsp freshly grated ginger
2 green onions, thinly sliced, white and green parts divided
1 tbsp toasted sesame oil
2½ tbsp toasted sesame seeds
1–2 heads broccoli (optional), blanched, to serve

FOR THE MARINADE

½ tbsp soy sauce
1 tbsp Shaoxing wine (or mirin, dry sherry, water, etc.)
¼ tsp white pepper (or black pepper)
1 tbsp cornstarch
¼ tsp baking soda (optional)
1 tbsp neutral-tasting oil
1 egg white

FOR THE SESAME CHICKEN SAUCE

½ tbsp soy sauce
1½ tbsp oyster sauce
2 tbsp granulated sugar
1 tbsp honey
1 tbsp white vinegar (or rice vinegar)
2 tbsp ketchup
1 tsp chicken bouillon powder
5 tbsp water
1 tbsp cornstarch

1. In a large bowl, combine all the marinade ingredients and toss the chicken pieces in the marinade until evenly coated. Cover with plastic wrap and marinate in the fridge for at least 10 minutes.
2. To make the sesame chicken sauce, in a small bowl, combine all the ingredients. Mix until thoroughly combined and set aside.
3. Add the potato starch (or cornstarch) to a big tray. Grab a piece of chicken and lightly coat the outside. Place the chicken piece on another tray. Repeat with the remaining chicken pieces.
4. In a large wok or heavy-bottomed pot, heat about 2 inches (5cm) of cooking oil to 340°F (170°C). Working in batches, carefully place the chicken pieces in the oil (dropping them away from you). Fry for 3 to 4 minutes or until light brown. Remove from the hot oil and place on a wire rack. Using a fine sieve, remove little bits that are left in the oil.
5. Increase the oil temperature to 355°F (180°C). Fry the chicken pieces a second time for 2 to 3 minutes until crispy and cooked through. Transfer to the wire rack and rest.
6. In another large wok or pan, heat 2 tablespoons of oil over medium-high heat. Once it gets nice and hot, add the garlic, ginger, and white parts of the green onions. Sauté for 30 seconds or until fragrant. Increase the heat to high, add the sesame chicken sauce, and give a good stir for 1 minute or until the sauce starts to thicken. Add the chicken and quickly toss together for 1 minute or until nicely coated. Turn off the heat. Add the sesame oil and sesame seeds. Give a final mix.
7. To serve, nicely arrange the blanched broccoli (if using) in a circle on a serving plate. Place the sesame chicken into that circle. Garnish with the green parts of the green onions. Serve and enjoy immediately.

NOTE: In Step 5, the oil can make a lot more noise and bubbles than during the first fry, but don't worry about it. That's natural. This double-frying technique will help remove all of the moisture from the crust and make it extra crispy.

EGG FRIED RICE

Fried Rice with Eggs

PREP TIME: **3 minutes** // COOK TIME: **7 minutes** // SERVES: **4**

Egg fried rice is one of the easiest fried rice dishes of all time, but at the same time, one of the greatest in the fried rice world.

5–6 large eggs
Small pinch of salt, plus more to season
4 tbsp neutral-tasting oil, divided
4 cups cooked and cooled white rice, preferably day-old jasmine rice
2½ tbsp soy sauce
3 green onions, thinly sliced
2 tsp toasted sesame oil (optional)

1. In a medium bowl, beat the eggs with the salt.
2. In a large wok or pan, heat 2 tablespoons of oil over high heat. Once it gets nice and hot, add the beaten eggs and cook for 30 seconds or until the bottom turns light brown. Flip and cook the other side for another 30 seconds or until it's lightly browned on the bottom.
3. Push the eggs to one side of the wok and add 2 tablespoons of oil to the empty space. Add the rice and move the eggs to the top of the rice. Using a spatula, break the rice and eggs up and stir-fry for 2 minutes or until they are evenly distributed.
4. Add the soy sauce around the sides of the wok and give it about 30 seconds to caramelize. Stir-fry for 2 minutes or until every single grain of rice is evenly coated. Taste and add salt if needed.
5. Turn the heat off. Add the green onions and sesame oil (if using). Give a final mix. Enjoy immediately.

CLAIRE SAYS:

This is Aaron's simplified version of egg fried rice, with the fewest ingredients and easiest steps. If you'd like to make fried rice closer to restaurant quality, try adding a pinch of MSG in Step 3, or use 1½ tablespoons of soy sauce and 1 tablespoon of oyster sauce instead of just the soy sauce. The result? You'll end up with a more flavorful version of egg fried rice.

CLAIRE SAYS:

As Aaron mentioned, this recipe is incredibly versatile and can be adapted to suit whatever you have in your fridge. So feel free to play around with different ingredients—it's all going to turn out amazing. Still feeling a bit intimidated? Then trying out some of our other fried rice variations on our YouTube channel or blog could be a great way to get started.

CHICKEN FRIED RICE

Fried Rice with Chicken

PREP TIME: **10 minutes + 20 minutes to marinate** // COOK TIME: **12 minutes** // SERVES: **4**

Are you sick and tired of greasy takeout fried rice or those expensive delivery fees? Then it's time to say goodbye to takeout and hello to homemade. This isn't just any fried rice recipe—trust me. Once you master this, you'll be able to create restaurant-quality fried rice with whatever ingredients you have at home, not just chicken. Yes, this recipe will become the ultimate guideline for any type of fried rice you want to make.

---

9 oz (250g) boneless skinless chicken thighs (or breasts), cut into bite-sized pieces
4 large eggs
Kosher salt, to taste
4 tbsp neutral-tasting oil, divided
3 garlic cloves, finely chopped
3 green onions, thinly sliced, white and green parts divided
4 cups cooked and cooled white rice, preferably day-old jasmine rice
¼ cup frozen peas (optional), blanched and drained
¼ cup frozen carrots (optional), blanched and drained
Generous pinch of toasted sesame seeds, to garnish
2 tsp toasted sesame oil

FOR THE MARINADE

1 tsp soy sauce
1 tsp Shaoxing wine (or mirin, dry sherry, water, etc.)
1 tsp cornstarch
1 tsp neutral-tasting oil
⅛ tsp white pepper (or black pepper)

FOR THE FRIED RICE SAUCE

2 tbsp soy sauce
1 tbsp Shaoxing wine (or mirin, dry sherry, water, etc.)
½ tbsp chicken bouillon powder
¼ tsp white pepper (or black pepper)

1. In a large bowl, combine all the marinade ingredients and toss the chicken pieces in the marinade until thoroughly coated. Cover with plastic wrap and marinate in the fridge for at least 20 minutes.
2. To make the fried rice sauce, in a small bowl, combine all the ingredients. Mix until thoroughly combined and set aside.
3. In a medium bowl, beat the eggs with a pinch of salt.
4. In a large wok or pan, heat 2 tablespoons of oil over high heat. Once it gets nice and hot, add the eggs and cook for 30 seconds or until the eggs are 70% cooked. Remove from the wok and set aside.
5. In the same wok, add 2 tablespoons of oil and heat over high heat. Once it's heated, add the marinated chicken in a single layer. Let sit for 2 minutes or until nicely browned on the bottom. Add the garlic and white parts of the green onions, and sauté for 1 to 2 minutes or until the chicken is cooked through and fragrant.
6. Add the rice to the wok. Using a spatula, break the rice up and stir-fry for 2 minutes or until every single grain of rice is evenly coated with the aromatic oil.
7. Add the fried rice sauce around the edges of the wok. Give it about 30 seconds to caramelize and then mix. Add the blanched peas and carrots, if using. Stir-fry everything together for 2 minutes or until everything is evenly coated.
8. Add the eggs back into the wok. Break into little pieces and toss together for 1 to 2 minutes or until everything is evenly distributed. Taste and add more salt, if needed.
9. Turn off the heat. Add the green parts of the green onions, sesame seeds, and sesame oil. Give a final mix. Serve immediately.

CASHEW CHICKEN

Stir-Fried Chicken with Cashews

PREP TIME: **20 minutes + 20 minutes to marinate** // COOK TIME: **20 minutes** // SERVES: **3–4**

Here's another insanely easy, life-changing chicken stir-fry recipe. Comments like, "I made this tonight, and it was incredibly delicious!" keep pouring in on our cashew chicken YouTube video. That's right—this saucy, flavorful chicken dish has truly changed their lives. Now, it's your turn.

---

1 lb (450g) boneless, skin-on chicken thighs (or breasts), cut into bite-sized pieces
2 tbsp neutral-tasting oil, plus more if needed
½ cup unsalted raw (or roasted) cashews
4 garlic cloves, finely chopped
½ tsp freshly grated ginger
3 green onions, the tops cut into 2-inch (5cm) pieces, plus thinly sliced white parts
½ yellow onion, diced
2 cups red, yellow, and green bell peppers, cut into bite-sized pieces

FOR THE MARINADE

½ tbsp soy sauce
½ tbsp Shaoxing wine (or mirin, dry sherry, water, etc.)
¼ tsp white pepper (or black pepper)
¼ tsp baking soda (optional)
1 tbsp cornstarch
1 tbsp neutral-tasting oil

FOR THE SAUCE

1 tbsp soy sauce
1 tbsp oyster sauce
½ tsp dark soy sauce
1 tbsp granulated sugar
¼ tsp white pepper (or black pepper)
1 tsp toasted sesame oil
4 tbsp water
1 tbsp cornstarch
1 tbsp chicken bouillon powder

1. In a large bowl, combine all the marinade ingredients and toss the chicken pieces in the marinade until evenly coated. Cover with plastic wrap and marinate in the fridge for at least 20 minutes.
2. To prepare the sauce, in a small bowl, whisk together all the ingredients until thoroughly combined. Set aside.
3. In a large wok or pan, heat the oil over medium heat. Once it gets nice and hot, add the cashews. Roast for 2 to 3 minutes or until deep dark brown. Stir constantly to prevent burning. Remove from the wok, leaving the oil behind.
4. Place the same wok over high heat. Once it's nice and hot, add the marinated chicken in a single layer. Let sear for 1 minute or until golden brown on the bottom. Flip and cook for 2 to 3 minutes or until cooked through. Remove from the wok and set aside.
5. Place the same wok over medium heat. Into the chicken fat, add the garlic, ginger, and white parts of the green onions, and sauté for 1 minute or until fragrant. (If there is not enough oil because you used chicken breast, you can add 1 or 2 tablespoons of oil.)
6. Increase the heat to high. Add the onion and bell peppers and stir-fry for 1 minute or until the vegetables are slightly cooked. Add the chicken back into the wok and toss together for 30 seconds or until the chicken pieces are coated with the aromatic oil.
7. Give the sauce a quick stir and add it to the wok. Stir everything together for 1 minute or until the sauce has thickened and looks shiny. Turn off the heat. Add the green onions and cashews and give a final mix. Serve with hot rice.

CLAIRE SAYS:

To elevate the flavor of this dish, it's best to use chicken thighs with the skin on. The rendered fat from the skin blends beautifully with the aromatics and the sauce, creating an irresistible depth of flavor.

CLAIRE SAYS:

The key to this recipe is the charred onions, which create an amazing wok hei—a delightful smoky flavor that makes it hard to believe you made this at home.

BEEF AND ONION STIR-FRY

Stir-Fried Beef with Onions

PREP TIME: **15 minutes + 20 minutes to marinate** // COOK TIME: **10 minutes** // SERVES: **3–4**

I often hear people say that stir-fry dishes are difficult to make. But that's absolutely not true. Stir-frying is actually very straightforward and doesn't require any secret magic cooking techniques or anything like that. With this recipe, success in your kitchen is guaranteed, and this tender beef and aromatic onion stir-fry will break that stereotype.

---

1 lb (450g) beef flank steak or any steak cut, sliced against the grain into ¼-inch (0.5cm) thick slices
2 tbsp neutral-tasting oil, divided
1¼ large yellow onions, cut into 1-inch (2.5cm) thick slices and layers separated
3 garlic cloves, finely chopped
2 tsp freshly grated ginger
3 green onions, the tops cut into 2-inch (5cm) pieces, plus thinly sliced white parts
⅓ carrot (60g), thinly sliced
1 tsp toasted sesame oil

FOR THE MARINADE

1 tbsp soy sauce
1 tbsp Shaoxing wine (or mirin, dry sherry, water, etc.)
¼ tsp white pepper (or black pepper)
1 tbsp cornstarch
¼ tsp baking soda
1 tbsp neutral-tasting oil

FOR THE SAUCE

1 tbsp soy sauce
2 tbsp oyster sauce
½ tsp dark soy sauce
1 tbsp granulated sugar
1 tbsp Shaoxing wine (or mirin, dry sherry, water, etc.)
1 tsp chicken bouillon powder
5 tbsp water
1 tbsp cornstarch

1. In a large bowl, combine all the marinade ingredients and toss the beef slices in the marinade until evenly coated. Cover with plastic wrap and marinate in the fridge for at least 20 minutes.
2. To prepare the sauce, in a small bowl, whisk together all the ingredients until thoroughly combined. Set aside.
3. In a large wok or pan, heat 1 tablespoon of oil over high heat. Once it's nice and hot, add the marinated beef in a single layer. Let sear for 1 minute or until golden brown on the bottom. Flip and cook for 1 to 2 minutes or until the beef is seared all over. Remove from the wok and set aside.
4. To the same wok, add 1 tablespoon of oil and heat over high heat. Once it's nice and hot, add the onions. Spread them out and let sit for 1 to 2 minutes or until nicely charred on the bottom.
5. Add the garlic, ginger, and white parts of the green onions, and sauté for 30 seconds or until fragrant. Add the beef, carrot, and sauce, and toss together for 1 minute or until the sauce has thickened and everything is coated well.
6. Turn off the heat. Add the sesame oil and the green parts of the green onions. Give a final mix. Serve with hot rice.

BLACK PEPPER BEEF

Stir-Fried Beef with Black Pepper Sauce

PREP TIME: **15 minutes + 20 minutes to marinate** // COOK TIME: **10 minutes** // SERVES: **3–4**

When I was young with a lack of experience in Chinese cuisine, I once visited a Chinese takeout restaurant alone. I'm not sure if they still use those kinds of menus, but back then, it was a vertically folded paper menu that listed, exaggerating just a bit here, around 300 dishes. I was completely overwhelmed by the number of options. Just as I began to panic, three words stood out like a beacon of hope: black pepper beef. Even then, I knew that would taste good. I don't even remember the name of that restaurant but that unforgettable flavor from that day is what inspired this recipe.

---

1 lb (450g) New York strip or tenderloin, sliced against the grain into ¼-inch (0.5cm) thick slices
2 tbsp neutral-tasting oil, divided
½ yellow onion, diced
1 green onion, thinly sliced
3 garlic cloves, finely chopped
2 tsp freshly grated ginger
1 green bell pepper, cut into bite-sized pieces
1 red bell pepper, cut into bite-sized pieces
1 tsp toasted sesame oil
1 tsp freshly cracked black pepper

FOR THE MARINADE

1 tbsp soy sauce
1 tbsp Shaoxing wine (or mirin, dry sherry, water, etc.)
½ tsp white pepper (or black pepper)
1 tbsp cornstarch
¼ tsp baking soda
1 tbsp neutral-tasting oil

FOR THE SAUCE

1 tbsp soy sauce
2 tbsp oyster sauce
½ tsp dark soy sauce (optional)
½ tbsp granulated sugar
1 tbsp Shaoxing wine (or mirin, dry sherry, water, etc.)
1 tsp chicken bouillon powder
5 tbsp water
1 tbsp cornstarch

1. In a large bowl, combine all the marinade ingredients and toss the beef slices in the marinade until evenly coated. Cover with plastic wrap and marinate in the fridge for at least 20 minutes.
2. To prepare the sauce, in a small bowl, whisk together all the ingredients until thoroughly combined. Set aside.
3. In a large wok or pan, heat 1 tablespoon of oil over high heat. Once it's nice and hot, add the marinated beef in a single layer. Let sear for 1 minute or until golden brown on the bottom. Flip and cook for 1 to 2 minutes or until the beef is seared all over. Remove from the wok and set aside.
4. To the same wok, add 1 tablespoon of oil and heat over high heat. Once it's nice and hot, add the onion. Spread them out and let sit for 1 to 2 minutes or until nicely charred on the bottom.
5. Add the green onion, garlic, and ginger, and sauté for 30 seconds or until fragrant. Add the bell peppers and stir-fry for 1 minute or until the vegetables are slightly cooked but still crunchy.
6. Add the beef. Give the sauce a quick stir and add it to the wok. Stir everything together for 1 minute or until the beef is evenly coated with the sauce and shiny.
7. Turn off the heat. Add the sesame oil and black pepper and give a final mix. Serve with hot rice.

CLAIRE SAYS:

I think the highlight of this dish is the crunchy texture of the bell peppers, which perfectly contrasts with the juicy, tender beef. So make sure to cook them quickly over high heat to keep their crunchiness. Also, rather than preparing it in advance, be sure to serve it immediately after cooking. The crunchiness of the bell peppers makes a huge difference in the overall flavor.

CLAIRE SAYS:

If you want to maximize the moist and fluffy texture of the eggs, try cooking them in Step 4 as if you're making a soft, slightly set omelet rather than scrambling them. This way, it'll feel like you're eating a cloud—like cotton candy.

TOMATO EGG STIR-FRY

Stir-Fried Tomatoes with Eggs

PREP TIME: **7 minutes** // COOK TIME: **10 minutes** // SERVES: **2–3**

At first glance, many people think this would be nothing special because it's just tomatoes and eggs. But after just one bite, everyone is surprised by the true symphony of flavors that this simplicity creates.

---

4 large eggs
¼ tsp kosher salt, plus more to season
Small pinch of granulated sugar
Small pinch of MSG (optional)
3 tbsp neutral-tasting oil, divided
1-2 green onions, thinly sliced, white and green parts divided
4 ripe medium-sized tomatoes, about 17 oz (500g) in total, cut into wedges
2 tbsp water
1 tbsp ketchup
½ tsp toasted sesame oil (optional)

FOR THE SAUCE

1 tsp soy sauce
1 tsp oyster sauce
1 tsp granulated sugar

FOR THE SLURRY

½ tbsp cornstarch
1 tbsp water

1. In a medium bowl, beat the eggs with the salt, sugar, and MSG (if using). Set aside.
2. To prepare the sauce, in a small bowl, whisk together all the ingredients until thoroughly combined. Set aside.
3. To make the slurry, in a small bowl, whisk together the cornstarch and water. Set aside.
4. In a large wok or pan, heat 2 tablespoons of oil over high heat. Once it gets nice and hot, pour in the beaten eggs. Gently move around and cook for 45 seconds. (You don't have to stir vigorously because if the eggs are broken up into pieces, they are more likely to get overcooked when they're mixed with the tomatoes later.) When the eggs are 80% cooked, remove from the wok and set aside.
5. To the same wok, add 1 tablespoon of oil and heat over high heat. Add the white parts of the green onions and sauté for 1 minute or until fragrant. Add the tomatoes, a pinch of salt, and the sauce. Stir-fry for 1 to 2 minutes or until the tomatoes are coated with the aromatic oil and the sauce.
6. Add the water and ketchup. Stir and simmer for 1 to 2 minutes. When the tomatoes have softened and the juices are bubbling, add the cornstarch slurry and stir for 30 seconds or until the juices have thickened.
7. Add the eggs back into the wok. Break them into smaller pieces and stir everything together for 1 minute. Taste and add more salt if needed. Add the sesame oil (if using) and give a final mix. Transfer to a serving plate and garnish with the green parts of the green onions. Serve with hot rice.

TOMATO EGG DROP SOUP

Chinese Tomato Soup with Eggs

PREP TIME: **7 minutes** // COOK TIME: **15 minutes** // SERVES: **2**

Tomatoes and eggs are a perfect combo, and it's no wonder so many cultures use this pairing in their dishes. Even though I didn't grow up eating this Chinese tomato egg drop soup, just a single sip of it made me believe that it is one of my favorite comfort foods of all time. And for your information, I'm Korean.

---

2 large eggs
Small pinch of salt, plus more to season
2 tbsp neutral-tasting oil
1 garlic clove, finely chopped
2 green onions, thinly sliced, white and green parts divided
½ tbsp soy sauce
2 ripe medium-sized tomatoes, about ½ lb (225g), cut into bite-sized pieces
3½ cups water
1 tbsp chicken bouillon powder
1½ tbsp ketchup
White pepper (or black pepper), to taste
½ tsp toasted sesame oil

FOR THE SLURRY

1 tbsp cornstarch
2 tbsp water

1. In a medium bowl, beat the eggs with the salt. Set aside.
2. To make the slurry, in a small bowl, whisk together the cornstarch and water. Set aside.
3. In a large wok or pot, heat the oil over medium-high heat. Once it gets nice and hot, add the garlic and white parts of the green onions. Sauté for 30 seconds or until fragrant. Add the soy sauce and stir for 20 seconds. (Be careful of oil splatter when you add the soy sauce.)
4. Add the tomatoes and stir-fry for 2 minutes. When the tomatoes have released their juices and start bubbling, add the water, chicken bouillon powder, and ketchup. Bring to a boil and simmer for 3 minutes.
5. Add salt and pepper to taste. Let simmer for 2 more minutes. Give the cornstarch slurry a quick stir and add it to the wok. Stir immediately until the soup is thickened.
6. Reduce the heat to medium. Slowly drizzle the beaten eggs into the soup in a thin stream. Turn off the heat and gently stir with a ladle to create lacy egg ribbons. Add the green parts of the green onions and sesame oil. Give a final mix. Serve immediately.

CLAIRE SAYS:

Don't rush to eat this soup, even though it looks incredibly delicious. The broth, thickened with the cornstarch slurry, slowly cools down, so it's much hotter than it seems, and you could easily burn yourself. Yes, I'm speaking from multiple personal experiences.

CLAIRE SAYS:

Aaron makes chow fun at home using a variety of proteins—chicken, pork, tofu, and even seafood. While the most classic version is made with beef, feel free to experiment with different protein options to create your favorite version. They'll all taste amazing!

BEEF CHOW FUN

Stir-Fried Flat Rice Noodles with Beef

PREP TIME: **30 minutes + 10 minutes to marinate** // COOK TIME: **8 minutes** // SERVES: **2**

Whenever Claire and I visit a dim sum place, we always order this Cantonese classic. Juicy, tender beef and chewy wide rice noodles with a pleasant, smoky, charred flavor from the wok. Honestly, I could visit that dim sum restaurant only for this and I'm sure many of you would agree. The classic beef chow fun uses fresh wide flat rice noodles, but for those who don't have easy access to them, this recipe uses dried rice noodles.

½ lb (225g) beef flank steak, thinly sliced against the grain
4 tbsp neutral-tasting oil, divided
½ yellow onion, thinly sliced
3 green onions, the tops cut into 2-inch (5cm) pieces, plus thinly sliced white parts
2 garlic cloves, finely chopped
7 oz (200g) dried rice noodles, soaked in warm water for 30 minutes to 1 hour until softened
1 cup mung bean sprouts
1 tsp toasted sesame oil
Kosher salt, to taste

FOR THE MARINADE

½ tbsp soy sauce
1 tsp dark soy sauce
1 tsp Shaoxing wine (or mirin, dry sherry, water, etc.)
¼ tsp baking soda
½ tbsp neutral-tasting oil
Small pinch of white pepper (or black pepper)
½ tbsp cornstarch

FOR THE CHOW FUN SAUCE

2 tbsp soy sauce
1 tbsp oyster sauce
1 tsp dark soy sauce
1 tbsp Shaoxing wine (or mirin, dry sherry, water, etc.)
2 tsp granulated sugar
¼ tsp white pepper (or black pepper)

1. In a large bowl, combine all the marinade ingredients and toss the beef slices in the marinade until evenly coated. Cover with plastic wrap and marinate in the fridge for at least 10 minutes.
2. To make the chow fun sauce, in a small bowl, combine all the ingredients. Mix until thoroughly combined and set aside.
3. In a large wok or pan, heat 2 tablespoons of oil over high heat. Once it's nice and hot, add the marinated beef in a single layer and sear for 30 seconds or until nicely browned. Flip and sear the other side for another 30 seconds or until browned. Remove from the wok and set aside.
4. Place the same wok over medium-high heat and add 2 tablespoons of oil. When it gets nice and hot, add the onion, white parts of the green onions, and garlic, and sauté for 30 seconds or until fragrant.
5. Increase the heat to high, add the drained noodles, and toss together for 30 seconds or until nicely coated with the aromatic oil. Spread the noodles evenly in the wok and let sear for 2 minutes or until slightly charred.
6. Add the sauce and stir-fry for 1 minute or until the noodles are evenly coated. Add the beef back in and toss everything together for 1 minute. Add the green parts of the green onions and mung bean sprouts and stir-fry for 30 seconds or until thoroughly combined.
7. Turn off the heat. Drizzle with the sesame oil and give a final mix. Taste and add salt if needed. Transfer to a serving plate and serve immediately.

SHRIMP TOAST

Deep-Fried Sandwich with Shrimp Filling

PREP TIME: **15 minutes** // COOK TIME: **15 minutes** // MAKES: **8**

Too many people seem to dislike seafood, and I think that's because they haven't had the opportunity to enjoy perfectly cooked seafood dishes from a young age. That's why I'm excited to share this dish with you. This crispy, golden-brown sandwich filled with minced shrimp offers the perfect balance of flavor and texture. Even if you (or your family) have avoided seafood for decades, you won't be able to say no to this bad boy. Trust me. This will be a good start.

---

9 oz (250g) peeled and deveined shrimp, patted dry and finely minced
2 tbsp potato starch (or cornstarch), plus more if needed
1 egg white
2 tbsp thinly sliced green onion
1 tsp chicken bouillon powder
Freshly cracked black pepper, to taste
1 tbsp unsalted butter, melted
4 slices white bread, cut into quarters with the crusts trimmed off
High-heat oil (such as canola, avocado, vegetable, etc.), for frying

FOR THE DIPPING SAUCE

1 tbsp oyster sauce
1 tbsp ketchup
1 tbsp white vinegar
½ tbsp granulated sugar
1 tbsp minced garlic

1. To make the dipping sauce, in a small bowl, combine all the ingredients. Mix until thoroughly combined. Set aside.
2. In a medium bowl, combine the minced shrimp, potato starch, egg white, green onion, chicken bouillon powder, black pepper, and butter. With a gloved hand, mix vigorously in one direction for 2 to 3 minutes or until it gets a little sticky. (If it's too watery, you can add a little bit more starch.)
3. Put a spoonful of shrimp filling on 8 of the bread slices and cover them with the remaining slices.
4. In a wok or heavy-bottomed pot, heat about 2 inches (5cm) of cooking oil to 320°F (160°C). Working in batches, carefully place the sandwiches in the oil. Fry for 6 minutes or until golden brown on both sides. Remove from the hot oil and drain on a wire rack or on some paper towels. Let rest for 2 minutes.
5. Transfer to a serving plate and serve with the dipping sauce.

CLAIRE SAYS:

Shrimp toast can feel a bit rich on its own. That's why you must pair it with Aaron's special dipping sauce. This garlicky, tangy, and sweet sauce will perfectly balance out the richness of the shrimp toast.

INDEX

H

I

J

K

R

S

ACKNOWLEDGMENTS

Thank you to everyone—subscribers, followers, supporters, and readers of this book. Without your encouragement, I couldn't have created this book. Your support has allowed me to keep doing what I love, and for that, I'm truly grateful. Thank you from the bottom of my heart. I owe it all to you.

Thank you to my team: Patrick Hwaseok Kim and Juno Park. Patrick, you have no idea how grateful I am to you. I truly appreciate the way you push me to do my best and always offer thoughtful advice when I need it most. Thank you for being such a steady source of support throughout this journey. Juno, I am always thankful for your brilliant work and quiet strength. Thanks to your steady and endless efforts behind the scenes, Aaron and Claire has grown into something truly special.

Thank you to Hyeseon Shin and everyone at Bombloombom photo studio. Without your incredible passion and effort, this book wouldn't have come together so beautifully. It was truly an honor to work with all of you once again.

Thank you to my dedicated publishing team—Brandon, Jessica, and everyone at DK for all the effort you put into this book. I'm deeply grateful for your dedication, insight, and the countless hours you devoted to bringing this book to life. Your expertise and advice helped make this the best book that it could be. Thank you.

Thank you to all of my friends from the restaurant industry. Because of your great feedback, the recipes in this book became easier to follow and more delicious. I can't name all of you here, but I'm sure you all know who you are. Thank you so much!

And finally, to my lady Claire. Thank you for your thoughtful feedback, endless encouragement, and for being by my side every step of the way. Even while preparing for the arrival of our soon-to-be-born son, you supported me in quiet but meaningful ways. Your love and belief in me have meant the world. I'm so lucky to have you. I love you.